# THE OLD ONES
## OF NEW MEXICO

*Robert Coles* is a child psychiatrist and writer. He went to New Mexico under a Ford Foundation grant in 1972 to work with Chicano children there. This book is the result of a series of interviews he held with the older residents of the area. Among Dr. Coles's many other books is the *Children of Crisis* series, Volumes 2 and 3 of which received a Pulitzer Prize in 1973.

*Alex Harris* is a 1971 graduate of Yale University, where he was a student of photographer Walker Evans. His photographs of rural Southerners were exhibited at the Carolina Symposium of the South, where he and Coles met. Harris now lives in a small Spanish village in northern New Mexico.

# ROBERT COLES

# THE OLD ONES
## OF NEW MEXICO

## Photographs by ALEX HARRIS

ANCHOR BOOKS
*Anchor Press/Doubleday*
*Garden City, New York   1975*

*The Old Ones of New Mexico* was published in a hardbound edition by University of New Mexico Press in 1973. The Anchor edition is published by arrangement with University of New Mexico Press.

Anchor Books edition: 1975
ISBN: 0-385-09900-2

*To the people who appear and speak
in this book, and to others like them
we have been privileged to meet and
come to know.*

# ACKNOWLEDGMENTS

Portions of this book have appeared in *The New Yorker, The American Poetry Review,* and *Commonweal.* I wish to thank the editors of those periodicals for the space they judged worth giving to these somewhat obscure people, not always considered worth the interest and favorable regard of other Americans. I also wish to thank Elizabeth Heist and Carl Mora of the University of New Mexico Press. Alex Harris and I have been offered much by the state of New Mexico. The state's university press has not only given our work sanction, but helped it out considerably, because the editors have known themselves who it is and what it is we have wanted to describe or evoke, and so have been especially thoughtful critics.

# CONTENTS

# INTRODUCTION

One mother after another urged me to pay special attention to the old people. Here is what one of them told me in December of 1972: "You should talk with the children's grandparents. You should tell the Anglos about our old men and women. With us the grandfather and the grandmother are very important. I see on television how the Anglos treat their old people: to the garbage heap they go. For me my parents and my husband's parents are the most important people in the world—along with our priest, of course."

I came to live in New Mexico in 1972 so that I could get to know the children: children of Spanish background as well as the children of the Pueblo Indians who live in large numbers north of Albuquerque. I had begun my work with Spanish-speaking children in Florida, where Chicanos now make up about one-third of the so-called Eastern stream of migrant farmworkers, traveling from Florida to Maine and back, year in, year out. In the 1960s I spent much time with such people, and I have written about what I saw and heard in the second volume of *Children of Crisis: Migrants, Sharecroppers, Mountaineers.* Many of the Chicano children I met on the Eastern seaboard had been born in Texas;

in search of a better life, their parents had left the Rio Grande Valley, where thousands of agricultural workers from Mexico live and work under extremely difficult and often oppressive circumstances. I began to visit the Rio Grande Valley—Texas towns like Edinburg, Crystal City, McAllen—in 1970. I had by then largely finished the work I have described in three volumes of *Children of Crisis,* and had decided to work more closely and at greater length with Chicano families.

In Texas I heard about New Mexico; often I was told that if I wanted to see a "different" kind of Spanish-speaking person, I had best move next door, to that state. So I eventually did, taking up residence in Albuquerque and from there traveling widely in all directions, especially to the east of the city, through the Sandia mountains, and up north to the highland country well above Santa Fe. In those areas one finds settlements of families headed for many generations by small farmers or ranchers. The people are strong, proud, vigorous, independent. They are of "Spanish" descent, yet can be called "old-line" Americans: they have been here far longer than many other well-established "groups." They have clung tenaciously to their own traditions and values, not the least of which is their language; they have by and large learned English, especially the younger people have, but they have kept fluent in Spanish. Apart from the language, they live in towns which often seem right out of Spain in appearance, and they retain customs and habits that are clearly Spanish: preferences for particular foods, ways of speaking to one another, religious attitudes, a view of life, really. Still, one has to note that the colonization of New Mexico—and other areas which made up the northern frontier of what was known from the sixteenth century through the mid-nineteenth century as "New Spain"—was largely accomplished by settlers from central Mexico. The conquerors were Spanish officers and mestizo soldiers—people of mixed Spanish and Indian blood, and in their wake came mestizo settlers who were thoroughly Hispanicized culturally.

As a child psychiatrist I have been trying to find out how that Hispanic view of life is transmitted to children and shapes for them a distinctive kind of experience—a childhood obviously, in certain respects, like that of other children around the world, but a childhood also quite unique. I have written this book in the midst of that study, and, I repeat, at the behest of a number of people I have been getting to know, not only the mothers but the priests. One priest stated the connection between the children and the old people most emphatically: "If you want to know about the children, you must first speak with the old people; what they believe, the child soon believes. The parents are go-betweens, I often think: they are very close to *their* parents, and hand down beliefs from the very old to the very young."

I protested to him. Isn't that always the case, even among the Anglos he often talks about? And besides, the priest himself was one of several quite old village curates of Spanish descent I'd met; perhaps he was feathering his own generation's cap. But over the months I was more than persuaded. I came to see how extraordinarily important these elderly men and women are in the lives of their children and grandchildren; I also came to see that, old as they are, there is a remarkable strength and vitality to them as human beings. Others from the Anglo world might consider them aloof, old-fashioned, superstitious, all too set in their ways. They themselves look upon their situation quite differently; they hold to certain values and assumptions, and, God willing, they will not forsake them.

I hope in the future to indicate how childhood goes

for New Mexico's Chicano children, who might also be referred to as American children of Spanish ancestry (and such descriptive words are treacherous, because different individuals or communities have their own definite preferences and prejudices as to what they ought be called). Here I hope to indicate something of what old age is like for people not always given the most attention or respect by the so-called dominant culture of this nation. I also hope to convey some of the strengths these aged men and women have managed to acquire over the many years of their lives. Over and over again in the medical and psychiatric literature and in books aimed at the general public one learns of the increasing sadness and even despair that come with old age: the body becomes more and more debilitated, and for that reason, as well as for those "socioeconomic" reasons we hear so much of, the elderly are described as having a thoroughly awful time of it. They not only feel weak and quite possibly in pain, they also feel ignored at best—and quite likely rebuffed or avoided like the plague.

Nor do I want to take issue with the observations of various psychological and sociological students of old age. There is no doubt that in this country old people are a threat of sorts: everyone wants to be young or look young—or at the very least, not be thought old and "out of it." The nation itself is young, as countries go, and its population is by no means old, relatively speaking. Moreover, the cult of youth is an established one in the United States—perhaps because so many people who have come here have felt the need to forsake their own cultural traditions. No matter what new attitudes replace those traditions, one thing has, alas, been evident: the immigrants must be succeeded by a generation of native-born Americans who are quite different—hence the development of an important split, one that has to do with language, customs, a whole sense of where loyalties belong and what a person ought to strive to obtain out of life.

In contrast, the families whose aged members I have been spending time with have not had to go through that kind of split—one that involves a difference of actual experience, followed by the onset of those ideological or philosophical rifts that often simply reflect various efforts at self-justification made by people who can no longer share certain assumptions about life. The old men and women this book aims to describe are not necessarily beyond the criticism of their children or grandchildren. Nor is it true that in New Mexico, if nowhere else in America, there is a thoroughly static society, a strict continuity of manners, convictions, articles of faith from one generation to the next. None of the old people I have worked with in New Mexico, or in any other part of the country, however contented or self-assured they seem, however honored by their families and friends and neighbors, have the idea that their children and grandchildren are extensions, pure and simple, of themselves in a generational progression that the Bible describes as "world without end." I have heard old men or women wish it could be that way: "I sometimes wonder why we can't be allowed to stay as we are; I have liked the life I have lived, and wanted the same kind of life for my sons and daughters, and for their sons and daughters. No such luck, though; the world presses down on us—even in this village it does, and I know we are removed up here in the mountains."

Such a wish is followed inevitably by the realization that there is just so much isolation a nation like this one allows even its more peripheral communities. And no doubt about it, these men and women, in their seventies or eighties, are Americans; they have lived through the

Great Depression of the 1930s, have seen their sons and grandsons leave to fight in the wars this country has fought, one after the other, in recent decades, have heard on the radio what the rest of us have heard. If they are old Spanish-speaking inhabitants of one state, they are also Americans who in many ways resemble others of their age elsewhere, regardless of racial or ethnic background. On the other hand, I believe they themselves express those qualities of mind, heart, and spirit that distinguish them from some of the rest of us.

A word or two about "method"—the way this "research" has been done. I have been visiting certain families, talking with them, trying to find out how they live and what they believe in. I make weekly, sometimes twice-weekly, calls, but have no standard questions in mind, no methodology to implement. I simply talk with my hosts at their leisure; whatever comes up, I am grateful to hear about. The men and women have spoken to me in both Spanish and English, often in one language for a spell, then in the other. They have all been *able* to speak English, even if haltingly at times; but I have encouraged them to speak in Spanish, and they have encouraged me to try my Spanish, which I would have to describe as broken or at best passable. I do believe, however, that I can understand the language fairly well. And I have made every effort to translate the speech I have heard in such a way that its flavor and tone come across to the middle-class "Anglo" people who will read this book.

A word about the photographs: Alex Harris is a friend of mine and a photographer who has spent time with migrant farmers and sharecroppers of the rural South as well as in New Mexico. He is the first person I have worked with as I have gone out on my visits—in contrast, that is, to joining a text of mine to pictures taken quite independently by a photographer. We both came to New Mexico under the same generous grant from the Ford Foundation, and we have shared our thoughts and impressions from week to week as we went about the state, trying to respond to its rich and unusual social and cultural life. He has wandered far and wide, and though his photographs are meant to dovetail with this text, they also represent his own attempt to do justice to the people he has met, and, I might add, become a friend of—a visitor anticipated and welcomed, in spite of all the amusing and puzzling equipment he necessarily has to bring along. The state of New Mexico has long fascinated photographers; its land, its skies, its flora and fauna, its hills and canyons, deserts and grazing lands, all have drawn attentive witnesses, who have come forth with much for us to see in exhibitions and books. But ironically the state's men and women and children are not so well known—too often they are overlooked. They deserve a photographer's respectful and thoughtful notice, and I believe that in the kind of observations he has recorded, Mr. Harris is a pioneer.

The people he presents here are not the people whose words I present, but they might well have been, because they are very similar in appearance and life-history, and in their faith. I cannot emphasize strongly enough my gratitude to this young and dedicated photographer-colleague of mine. If I have learned a lot from listening to the people about to have their say on this book's pages, I have also learned so very much from looking at Alex Harris's photographs and talking with him about what he has seen and heard. This book is our joint effort to set down some of our observations —observations made almost accidentally: we set out to come to children and were directed by them and their parents to grandparents—a rather interesting turn of events to happen these days. This book is also a statement of our own, as well as one about others; we have grown to admire and respect the people whose lives and fate we make a particular effort to portray in the following pages, and if some of our affection comes across, some of our gratitude, too, as well as a number of "facts" or "impressions" or "ideas," then it will have been an effort well worth making.

# 1

# TWO LANGUAGES, ONE SOUL

The Spanish-speaking people of the Southwest continue to be considered one of this nation's "problems," and for understandable reasons. In large measure they are poor, and their lot has by no means improved universally in recent years, for all the steps taken in the 1960s to make life easier for our so-called minorities. In the Rio Grande Valley of Texas even the vote cannot be taken for granted by many Mexican Americans, as they are called there. In the barrios of Los Angeles the "brown berets"—one more term—struggle on behalf of people plagued by joblessness and a host of discriminatory practices. "Chicano power!" one hears— yet another phrase; and looking at the power others have, it is not easy to disagree with the exhortation. In New Mexico there are distinct differences; unlike Texas or California, the state has long been responsive to its Spanish-speaking people. In fact, along with the Indians, they made up its "first families," and to this day, despite Anglo political and economic dominance, Spanish surnames are to be found everywhere: among holders of high political office, in the business world and the professions, and among storekeepers, small landowners, and blue-collar workers. Such a state of affairs has to be contrasted with conditions in Texas, where thousands of "Mexicanos" (as "gringos" sometimes

1

call them with barely concealed disdain) are either migrant farmworkers or go jobless, or in California, where César Chávez continues his not altogether successful struggle, and where "Latinos" (one hears that word used, too) share with blacks all the misery of the urban ghetto, most especially the sense that there is no one very important to call upon for help.

Still, even in New Mexico there is no reason to rejoice at the position the state's Spanish-speaking people occupy—especially when one compares it with the social and economic condition of Anglos. In many towns and villages those who speak Spanish are desperately poor; they lack work, or, if they do have jobs, they are menial ones, the only kind available. In the schools their children are often enough treated badly; reprimanded for using Spanish words, told that they are not suited for school, and made to feel that they will soon enough be living the same circumscribed lives their parents have known. Many who want better for the poor and struggle on their behalf—whether for the Anglo poor, black poor, Spanish-speaking poor—know how particularly destructive that kind of educational experience can be for young children, whose whole sense of "expectation" (What do I dare see ahead for myself, aim at, hope for?) is so crucially determined by the atmosphere in the elementary school.

Efforts to improve the condition of the Spanish-speaking poor of New Mexico have been predominantly educational. No one in the state has difficulty in voting, and the economy is unfortunately not advanced enough for those on the bottom to have any great success in demanding a larger share of the available wealth. Businesses are very much being courted, not with quite the desperation one sees in Alabama or Mississippi, but with a certain grim determination. And labor unions are not the power they are in Michigan or

Pennsylvania. But the schools have traditionally been the hope for the future all over this country; and they lend themselves more easily to change than a newly arrived factory or a firmly entrenched political hierarchy. So, one hears about "culturally disadvantaged" children and "culturally deprived" children; and among those both more knowledgeable and less given to condescension, "bilingual" education. Such terms are meant to convey the difficulties Spanish-speaking people have as outsiders of sorts. "America is Anglo," one hears Indian and Chicano children say in various parts of the Southwest, and that is that.

At least those children are granted a degree of hope by those of us who spend our time making judgments about the fate or destiny of one or another racial or ethnic group: they are young; changes are taking place; their lives will be less shame-ridden, more fulfilled. There are "job opportunity" programs. There are also various "enrichment" programs in the schools. Spanish is now increasingly allowed in those schools—to be spoken, even to be used by teachers. In the words of one Chicana social worker I have talked with: "We are determined to move ahead, even if there is great resistance from the power structure. No longer will Chicanos in New Mexico grow up feeling like second-class citizens. No longer will they feel misunderstood or scorned. In the old days they received the worst kind of schooling. They were made to feel stupid and awkward. They were made to feel they have nothing worthwhile to say or contribute. The Anglo teachers, the Anglo-run school system looked down on Chicanos. We were given no credit for our own values, for our culture and traditions. And the contempt showed on the people; they felt ashamed, inferior. They never learned to speak English the way the teachers did. They never learned to express themselves in school and they dropped out soon, usually well before high school was over. We hope to change that. We can't do anything about what has already happened. The old people are the way they are—it is too late for them to change. But it will be different for the young. They will have pride in themselves, and they will not only think well of themselves, but speak well. They won't have memories of Anglo teachers laughing at their Spanish, or punishing them for using it. They will speak Spanish with joy."

As she said, "the old people are the way they are." But exactly how is their "way" to be characterized? That is to say, how badly have they been scarred by the awful conditions described so forcefully by this particular political activist, among others? No doubt she is right—down to the last detail of her remarks; in recent years I have seen enough first-hand to more than confirm the basis for her sense of outrage. Still, I have to think of the people I have come to know in New Mexico—the old, thoroughly poor, certainly rather uneducated people, who have lived the hard, tough, sometimes terribly sad lives that the Chicana just quoted describes, and yet don't quite feel as she does about themselves. Nor do they speak as if they have been systematically brutalized, robbed of all their "self-esteem," as social scientists put it. In their seventies or eighties, with long memories of hardships faced and perhaps only partially (if at all) surmounted, "deprived" of education, made to feel hopelessly inarticulate, and obviously out of "the American mainstream," they are nevertheless men and women who seem to have held on stubbornly to a most peculiar notion: that they are eminently valuable and important human beings, utterly worth the respect, even admiration, not to mention the love, of their children and grandchildren.

Moreover, they are men and women who, for all the education they lack, all the wrongheaded or just plain

4

mean teachers they once ran up against, all the cultural bias and social discrimination they may have sensed or experienced outright, still manage not only to feel fairly assured about themselves as human beings, put here by the Lord for His own purposes, but also to say rather a lot about what is on their mind—and in such a way that they make themselves unmistakably clear. In fact, I have found myself at times overwhelmed by the power of their speech, the force that their language possesses, the dramatic expressions they call upon, the strong and subtle imagery available to them, the sense of irony and ambiguity they repeatedly and almost as a matter of course demonstrate. Perhaps my surprise and admiration indicate my own previous blind spots, my own ignorance and even prejudice. If so, I have been more than brought up short again and again.

Here are the words of an elderly woman who has had virtually no schooling and speaks a mixture of Spanish (which I have translated) and terse but forceful English. She lives in a small, isolated mountain community well to the north of Santa Fe and enjoys talking with her visitor: "Sometimes I have a moment to think. I look back and wonder where all the time has gone to —so many years; I cannot say I like to be reminded how many. My sister is three years older, eighty this May. She is glad to talk of her age. I don't like to mention mine. Maybe I have not her faith in God. She makes her way every day to church. I go only on Sundays. Enough is enough; besides, I don't like the priest. He points his finger too much. He likes to accuse us— each week it is a different sin he charges us with. My mother used to read me Christ's words when I was a girl—from the old Spanish Bible her grandmother gave to her on her deathbed. I learned that Christ was a kind man; He tried to think well of people, even the lowest

5

of the low, even those at the very bottom who are in a swamp and don't know how to get out, let alone find for themselves some high, dry land.

"But this priest of ours gives no one the benefit of the doubt. I have no right to find fault with him; I know that. Who am I to do so? I am simply an old lady, and I had better watch out: the Lord no doubt punishes those who disagree with His priests. But our old priest who died last year was so much finer, so much better to hear on a warm Sunday morning. Every once in a while he would even lead us outside to the courtyard and talk with us there, give us a second sermon. I felt so much better for listening to him. He was not in love with the sound of his own voice, as this new priest is. He did not stop and listen to the echo of his words. He did not brush away dust from his coat, or worry if the wind went through his hair. He was not always looking for a paper towel to wipe his shoes. My husband says he will buy this priest a dozen handkerchiefs and tell him they are to be used for his shoes only. Here when we get rain we are grateful, and it is not too high a price to pay, a little mud to walk through. Better mud that sticks than dust that blows away.

"Well, I should not go on so long about a vain man. We all like to catch ourselves in the mirror and find ourselves good to look at. Here I am, speaking ill of him, yet I won't let my family celebrate my birthdays any more; and when I look at myself in the mirror a feeling of sadness comes over me. I pull at my skin and try to erase the lines, but no luck. I think back: all those years when my husband and I were young, and never worried about our health, our strength, our appearance. I don't say we always do now; but there are times when we look like ghosts of ourselves. I will see my husband noticing how weak and tired I have become, how hunched over. I pretend not to see, but once

6

the eyes have caught something, one cannot shake the picture off. And I look at him, too; he will straighten up when he feels my glance strike him, and I quickly move away. Too late, though; he has been told by me, without a word spoken, that he is old, and I am old, and that is our fate, to live through these last years.

"But it is not only pity we feel for ourselves. A few drops of rain and I feel grateful; the air is so fresh afterwards. I love to sit in the sun. We have the sun so often here, a regular visitor, a friend one can expect to see often and trust. I like to make tea for my husband and me. At midday we take our tea outside and sit on our bench, our backs against the wall of the house. Neither of us wants pillows; I tell my daughters and sons that they are soft—those beach chairs of theirs. Imagine beach chairs here in New Mexico, so far from any ocean! The bench feels strong to us, not uncomfortable. The tea warms us inside, the sun on the outside. I joke with my husband; I say we are part of the house: the adobe gets baked, and so do we. For the most part we say nothing, though. It is enough to sit and be part of God's world. We hear the birds talking to each other, and are grateful they come as close to us as they do; all the more reason to keep our tongues still and hold ourselves in one place. We listen to cars going by and wonder who is rushing off. A car to us is a mystery. The young understand a car. They cannot imagine themselves not driving. They have not the interest we had in horses. Who is to compare one lifetime with another, but a horse is alive and one loves a horse and is loved by a horse. Cars come and go so fast. One year they command all eyes. The next year they are a cause for shame. The third year they must be thrown away without the slightest regret. I may exaggerate, but not much!

"My moods are like the church bell on Sunday: way

7

up, then down, then up again—and often just as fast. I make noises, too; my husband says he can hear me smiling and hear me turning sour. When I am sour I am really sour—sweet milk turned bad. Nothing pleases me. I am more selfish than my sister. She bends with the wind. I push my heels into the ground and won't budge. I know enough to frown at myself, but not enough to change. There was a time when I tried hard. I would talk to myself as if I was the priest. I would promise myself that tomorrow I would be different. I suppose only men and women can fool themselves that way; an animal knows better. Animals are themselves. We are always trying to be better—and often we end up even worse than we were to start with.

"But now, during the last moments of life, I think I have learned a little wisdom. I can go for days without an upset. I think I dislike our priest because he reminds me of myself. I have his long forefinger, and I can clench my fist like him and pound the table and pour vinegar on people with my remarks. It is no good to be like that. A man is lucky; it is in his nature to fight or preach. A woman should be peaceful. My mother used to say all begins the day we are born: some are born on a clear, warm day; some when it is cloudy and stormy. So, it is a consolation to find myself easy to live with these days. And I have found an answer to the few moods I still get. When I have come back from giving the horses each a cube or two of sugar, I give myself the same. I am an old horse who needs something sweet to give her more faith in life!

"The other day I thought I was going to say good-bye to this world. I was hanging up some clothes to dry. I love to do that, then stand back and watch and listen to the wind go through the socks or the pants or the dress, and see the sun warm them and make them smell fresh. I had dropped a few clothespins, and was picking them up, when suddenly I could not catch my breath, and a sharp pain seized me over my chest. I tried hard to stand up, but I couldn't. I wanted to scream but I knew there was no one nearby to hear. My husband had gone to the store. I sat down on the ground and waited. It was strong, the pain; and there was no one to tell about it. I felt as if someone had lassoed me and was pulling the rope tighter and tighter. Well here you are, an old cow, being taken in by the good Lord; that is what I thought.

"I looked at myself, sitting on the ground. For a second I was my old self again—worrying about how I must have appeared there, worrying about my dress, how dirty it would get to be. This is no place for an old lady, I thought—only for one of my little grandchildren, who love to play out here, build their castles of dirt, wetted down with water I give to them. Then more pain; I thought I had about a minute of life left. I said my prayers. I said goodbye to the house. I pictured my husband in my mind: fifty-seven years of marriage. Such a good man! I said to myself that I might not see him ever again; surely God would take him into Heaven, but as for me, I have no right to expect that outcome. Then I looked up to the sky and waited.

"My eye caught sight of a cloud. It was darker than the rest. It was alone. It was coming my way. The hand of God, I was sure of it! So that is how one dies. All my life, in the spare moments a person has, I wondered how I would go. Now I knew. Now I was ready. I thought I would soon be taken up to the cloud and across the sky I would go, and that would be that. But the cloud kept moving, and soon it was no longer above me, but beyond me; and I was still on my own land, so dear to me, so familiar after all these years. I can't be dead, I thought to myself, if I am here and the cloud is way over there, and getting further each second. Maybe the next cloud—but by then I had decided God had other things to do. Perhaps my name had come up, but He had decided to call others before me, and get around to me later. Who can ever know His reasons? Then I spotted my neighbor walking down the road, and I said to myself that I would shout for him. I did, and he heard. But you know, by the time he came I had sprung myself free. Yes, that is right, the pain was all gone.

"He helped me up, and he was ready to go find my husband and bring him back. No, I told him, no; I was all right, and I did not want to risk frightening my husband. He is excitable. He might get some kind of attack himself. I went inside and put myself down on our bed and waited. For an hour—it was that long, I am sure— my eyes stared at the ceiling, held on to it for dear life. I thought of what my life had been like: a simple life, not a very important one, maybe an unnecessary one. I am sure there are better people, men and women all over the world, who have done more for their neighbors and yet not lived as long as I have. I felt ashamed for a few minutes: all the complaints I'd made to myself and to my family, when the truth has been that my fate has been to live a long and healthy life, to have a good and loyal husband, and to bring two sons and three daughters into this world. I thought of the five children we had lost, three before they had a chance to take a breath. I wondered where in the universe they were. In the evening sometimes, when I go to close loose doors that otherwise complain loudly all night, I am likely to look at the stars and feel my long-gone infants near at hand. They are far off, I know; but in my mind they have become those stars—very small, but shining there bravely, no matter how cold it is so far up. If the stars have courage, we ought to have courage; that is what I was thinking, as I so often have in the past—and just then he was there, my husband, calling my name and soon looking into my eyes with his.

"I'm all right, I told him. He didn't know what had happened; our neighbor had sealed his lips, as I told him to do. But my husband knows me, so he knew I looked unusually tired; and he couldn't be easily tricked by me. The more I told him I'd just worked too hard, that is all, the more he knew I was holding something back. Finally, I pulled my ace card. I pretended to be upset by his questions and by all the attention he was giving me. I accused him: why do you make me want to cry, why do you wish me ill, with those terrible thoughts of yours? I am not ill! If you cannot let me rest without thinking I am, then God have mercy on you for having such an imagination! God have mercy! With the second plea to our Lord, he was beaten and silent. He left me alone. I was about to beg him to come back, beg his forgiveness. But I did not want him to bear the burden of knowing; he would not rest easy by day or by night. This way he can say to himself: she has always been cranky, and she will always be cranky, so thank God her black moods come only now and then—a spell followed by the bright sun again.

"I will say what I think happened: I came near going, then there was a change of heart up there in Heaven, so I have a few more days, or weeks, or months, or years—who knows? As for a doctor, I have never seen one, so why start now? Here we are so far away from a hospital. We have no money. Anglos don't like us, anyway: we are the poor ones, the lost ones. My son tells me the Anglos look down on us—old people without education and up in the hills, trying to scrape what we can from the land, and helped only by our animals. No matter; our son is proud of us. He is proud to stay here with us. He says that if he went to the city he would beg for work and be told no, no, no:

11

eventually he might be permitted to sweep someone's floor. Better to hold on to one's land. Better to fight it out with the weather and the animals.

"Again I say it: doctors are for others. My mother and my aunt delivered my children. I once went to see a nurse; she worked for the school and she told me about my children—the diseases they get. Thank you, I said. Imagine: she thought I knew nothing about bringing up children, or about the obstacles God puts in their way to test them and make them stronger for having gone through a fever, a rash, some pain. No, I will see no nurse and no doctor. They are as far from here as the stars. Oh, that is wrong; they are much farther. The stars I know and recognize and even call by name. They are my names, of course; I don't know what others call the stars. Is it wrong to do that? Perhaps I should ask the priest. Perhaps the stars are God's to name, not ours to treat like pets—by addressing them familiarly. But it is too late; my sins have been recorded, and I will soon enough pay for each and every one of them."

True, I have pulled together remarks made over a stretch of months. And again, I have translated her Spanish into plain, understandable English, or at least I hope I have done so. I have even "cleaned up" her English to an extent; that is, I have eliminated some of the repetitive words or phrases she uses—as we all do when we talk informally to visitors in our homes. On the other hand, I have made every effort to keep faithful to the spirit, and mostly to the letter, of her remarks. I have found that her Spanish is as bare, unaffected, and strong as her English. I have found that in both languages she struggles not only to convey meaning, but to enliven her words with her heart's burden or satisfactions. I have found that she struggles not only with her mind but with her body, her whole being, to express herself. Nor is she unique, some peculiar or specially gifted person whose manner of expression is thoroughly idiosyncratic. She certainly can be saddled with negatives, however compelling her way of speaking. She is uneducated. She is superstitious. She has never attended any bilingual classes. She is poor. Maybe some doctor would find her at times forgetful, a little "senile." She and others like her are rural people; they belong to a social and economic "system" that we all know is "out of date," because the future of America is to be found in cities like Albuquerque and their suburbs. Or so we are told.

Nor is she saintly. She can be morose, and at times quite cranky and reticent. Once she asked me, "What is the point of trying to talk to those who are deaf?" She had in mind some Anglo county officials who refused to give food stamps to a needy cousin of hers. She had in mind an Anglo teacher or two, and yes, a Spanish-speaking teacher or two; they had said rude things to her grandchildren and to their parents, her children. So, she becomes bitter and tense, and after a while she explodes. She admits it is not in her nature to hold in her beliefs, her feelings. She must have her say. And when she does her hands move, her body sways a bit, and sometimes, when she is especially worked up, there is a lurch forward from the chair, so that suddenly she is standing—giving a sermon, almost like the priests she has listened to all these years. A hand goes out, then is withdrawn. The head goes up, then is lowered. A step is taken forward, then back she goes—and soon she is seated again, ready to sew and continue the conversation on a less intense level. When she searches for a word, be it in Spanish or English, she drops her needle and thread, drops a fork or spoon, drops anything she may have in her hands. She

13

needs those old, arthritic fingers of hers. They flex and unflex; it is as if before her is a sandpile of words, and she must push and probe her way through it until she has found what she is looking for. Then the fingers can stop, the hands can relax and go back to other business, or simply be allowed a rest on her lap.

The more time I spend with this woman and her husband and their friends and neighbors and relatives, the more confused I become by much of what I read about them and their so-called cultural disadvantage. I have no inclination to turn such people into utterly flawless human beings, to create yet another highly romanticized group that can be used as a bludgeon against the rest of the country. They can be mean and narrow at times; the woman I have been quoting says things about hippies, and even, at times, about Anglos, that I disagree with or find exaggerated, unfair, distorted. As for her own disposition, she is clearly aware of her personal limitations. Still, she and her kind are at best pitied by many who have described their "plight." If there are grounds for pity (poverty, substantial unemployment, a degree of prejudice even in New Mexico, never mind Texas or California), there are also grounds for respect and admiration—maybe even envy. Some of us who have gone through all those schools and colleges and graduate schools, who have plenty of work and who live comfortable upper-middle-class lives, might want to stop and think about how *we* talk.

Occasionally I come home from a day spent with Chicano families or Indian families and pick up a psychiatric journal, or for that matter, the daily newspaper. Or I happen to go to a professional meeting and hear papers presented, or, afterwards, people talking in lobbies or corridors or restaurants—all those words, all those ideas, spoken by men and women who have no doubt about their importance, the value of their

14

achievements, and certainly not about their ability to "communicate." No one is proposing that jargon-spewing scholars of one sort or another overcome their "cultural disadvantage." Few are examining closely the rhetoric of various business and professional people, or that of their elected leaders—the phony, deceiving, dull, dreary, ponderous, smug, deadly words and phrases such people use and use and use. Relatively few are looking at the way such people are taught in elementary school and high school and beyond. Who is to be pitied, the old lady who can't recognize a possible coronary seizure and instead sees the hand of God approaching her, or some of us who jabber with our clichés and don't have the slightest idea how to use a metaphor or an image in our speech?

True, we have no "illusions"; we are educated, and pain in the chest is for us pain in the chest. Nor do we get carried away with ourselves; we are as sober as can be—so sober the whole world trembles at what we as the owners of this nation can do and have done amid our sobriety, our controlled speech and controlled actions. No hysteria for us. No gesticulations. No demonstration of exuberance, passion, heartiness, excitability. We are cool, calculating; we keep under wraps whatever spirit we have left, if any. And no doubt about it, the grandchildren mentioned so often by this particular old lady are not going to be like her: they are learning in school all sorts of valuable information—but also how to curb their imaginations, restrain their lively interest in harnessing language to the mind's rush of ideas, the heart's movements.

Their grandmother, soon to die, she knows, has said it far more precisely than I can—if with unintended irony: "My grandchildren will not struggle as I do to make myself clear. They are being fed words, Anglo words, by their teachers. They are learning the Spanish language; I only speak it, I don't know how to pick it apart! My oldest granddaughter showed me a book; it was about the Spanish language. I told her she does not need it; she can speak Spanish quite well. No, she said, she has to learn more, and the same with English. Who am I to disagree? Children have so much to learn. The better they can speak, the better it is for them. My grandchildren will speak better Spanish than I; and they will be good at English, too. There is change; there is progress. I am grateful. When I wonder whether there is any hope for my people, I look at my children's children and I say to myself: yes, there is hope. My husband says he hears the little ones chattering away: back and forth they go, from Spanish to English and then to Spanish again. I tell him that we haven't done so bad ourselves; we can make ourselves understood in both languages. But he says—and he is right—that it is not the struggle for them that it has been for us. There is enough struggle for any of us in this world; so, the less the better.

"I only worry that the more people have, the less grateful they feel to God. I know, because a while back, when we had an even harder time than now, we prayed to Him more often. Now our stomachs are full, our children give us money—not a lot, because they don't have much themselves, but some; and the result is that we ignore Him, or we only thank Him on Sundays, when we are in church. I have always felt that He listens more to our daily prayers at home, rather than those we offer in church, when it is a mere habit being practiced. But I am speaking out of turn; I have no right to speak for Him! He knows which prayers mean the most to Him. I have no right to feel sorry for my grandchildren, either. There are moments when I wish they put more of themselves into their fine English and their fine Spanish, but misery likes company, I guess.

My husband and I reach out, cry out, for our words, and we are so surprised at the little ones: what we can never take for granted, they have in such large supply. No wonder they have other things to think about than how to get their message across to people! No Anglo is going to make them feel speechless. I can't say I've felt speechless with Anglos, either; but I am sure that they have looked down on me, or not understood my English. As for my Spanish, it has served me well. The Anglos don't understand it, and a Spanish gentleman, one of great learning, would no doubt feel sorry for me, the way I use his language. But I repeat, it has served me well, the way I talk; that is as much as I can say, no more.

"Well, I do have another thought to offer. My daughter told me the other day that all our lives we have been split: we are Spanish, but we are Americans; we have our Spanish language, but in this country the Anglos are kings, and everyone has to speak their English or pay the penalties. I could not disagree. I took my daughter to me and told her she was right to listen to those teachers. I only worry that she and her children will take the message too seriously—will feel ashamed of their own parents, their own people's history. After all, even if there has been trouble, there has been God's grace: He has helped us; He has healed us; He has enabled us to try to be worthwhile and decent people. We have two languages, I know. We are in the middle; we don't know where to go, who to turn to. Or is it that we turn in one direction, then another? But God has given each of us a soul, and it is the soul that really counts. I do not have a Spanish soul, or a soul that is part Anglo. The soul is the place where each of us, no matter what language we speak, no matter our color, meets the Creator. We live the best we know how to live, and our actions are words to God, and He makes

17

His judgment. Through our soul we speak to Him and He to us. Oh, I am not very clear today! This is the end of my life, the month of December for me; and I fear my talk shows it! I only want to say that even though there are two languages to speak, there is only one soul. But maybe the time has come for me to stop speaking in any language. The soul finally tires of the body; it is a prison, and the soul wants to leave. Words struggle to leave us, but once spoken they are dead. The soul leaves and lives forever. I believe it does. I hope it does."

She makes that last distinction between faith and hope rather innocently. Not for her a dramatic division: I want something to be, but I'm not sure my wish will be realized; and so there is my religious conviction as opposed to my intuitive sense that one cannot be certain by any means. As for those words she mentions, they do indeed struggle for expression. She knows all the pain of the translator. She knows she has one range of expression given her by the Spanish language and another that is set by the English she uses. She moves back and forth, calls upon words and phrases and expressions and proverbs and sayings she has gathered together over the decades and made into her own particular way of both thinking and speaking. Who can (who wants to?) titrate the mixture, resort to percentages or long analytic statements about which idiom makes for what degree of her "pattern" of speech? In each home I visit, the language differs; it all depends on so much—a particular person's manner of getting on with people, a person's responsiveness to sounds (in contrast, say, to visual images), a person's experiences as a worker, a host of accidents and incidents and encounters that may have caused one person to be more talkative, more expansive, more sensitive to the requirements of "bilingual" life than others turn out to be. (A kind Anglo boss, for instance, who took pains once to offer some help with pronunciation, or with the mysteries of a given phrase of construction; or a priest who is especially devoted to the life of a parishioner, including his or her interest in self-expression; or a teacher who was encouraging rather than intimidating.)

Beyond all those "variables" there is the daily rhythm of a given kind of living—close to the land, in touch with nature, very much part of a community's collective experience. We who have become locked up in city apartments or small suburban lots may find the language of an old "illiterate" grandmother—from a settlement in north central New Mexico too small even to qualify as a village—unusually vivid or figurative. The fact is that such a woman has her heritage, her surroundings, her everyday experience, even as we have ours—hence the difference in language. But the power is ours, and also the numbers—we are the vast majority. Moreover, historically America is a "melting pot"; there is, there has been all along, the expectation that those who come here, or for that matter (the gall!) were here before anyone else, respond to the nation's "manifest destiny"—and such a destiny has its cultural as well as its brute military or political components. Meanwhile that woman and thousands like her, old and tired, proud and energetic, do what we all try to do: look at the world, listen to its sounds, figure out its outlines, its structure, its significance. Then comes that attempt at coherence which is language—and with it the connections that words provide: one person to another, the two of them to a neighborhood, and beyond.

There is no point holding up anyone's struggle with language as a standard by which others must measure themselves. I have probably not emphasized strongly enough the silences I have heard, the almost desperate search for words which quite frequently turns out to be unsuccessful. I am myself a writer, hence wordy. And my work makes me utterly dependent on the words of others—or at least when I write up that work I have to come forth with those words. The point is not to deny her wish—at least for her grandchildren, if not herself—to speak better, more fluent, English, maybe even a "higher" form of Spanish, too. The point is simply to emphasize the particularity and complexity of her life; and, not least, its integrity.

Against considerable odds she and her husband have carved out a "moment" for themselves on this earth. They happen to be alert, vigorous, stubborn people. They don't let things go; their ears prick up, their eyes dart, they love to smell food as well as taste it, and they enjoy touching people, objects, animals. They possess adequate if not superior intelligence. That being the case, for all their cultural and educational "deficits," for all the "handicaps" they have had to face, for all the difficulties of a "bilingual" life, they nevertheless prove themselves altogether adequate to the demands of their day-to-day existence. They make themselves known. They affirm themselves. They speak out of their minds and hearts. They reveal once again that a lean and willing soul can find its own carefully chosen if hesitantly uttered words, even as others, grown fat and sassy spiritually, can pour forth statements and remarks but worry little about what they sound like. After all, there is so much to lay claim upon through words, there are so many people to keep up with and impress and win over or argue down—rather than, as is the case with the woman I have quoted, simply reach and arouse and stir.

# 2

# UNA ANCIANA

He is eighty-three years old. Once he was measured as exactly six feet tall, but that was a half a century ago. He is sure that he has lost at least an inch or two. Sometimes, when his wife has grown impatient with his slouch, and told him to straighten up, he does her suggestion one better and tilts himself backward. Now are you happy? he seems to be asking her, and she smiles indulgently. His wife is also eighty-three. She always defers to her husband. She will not speak until he has had his say. She insists that he be introduced first to strangers. As the two of them approach a door, she makes a quick motion toward it, holds it patiently, and sometimes, if he is distracted by a conversation and slow to move through, one of her hands reaches for his elbow, while the other points: Go now, is the unstated message, so that I can follow.

They were born within a mile and within two months of one another in Cordova, New Mexico, in the north central part of the state. They are old Americans not only by virtue of age but by ancestry. For many generations their ancestors have lived in territory that is now part of the United States. Before the Declaration of Independence was written there were people not so far away from Cordova named Garcia living as they do, off the land. They are not, however, model citizens of their country. They have never voted, and no doubt the men who framed the Declaration of Independence would not be impressed by the boredom or indifference these New Mexicans demonstrate when the subject of politics comes up. They don't even make an effort to keep abreast of the news, though they do have a television set in their small adobe house. When Walter Cronkite or John Chancellor appears, neither of the Garcias listens very hard. For that matter, no programs really engage their undivided attention—and at first one is tempted to think them partially deaf. But the issue is taste, not the effects of age. Mrs. Garcia does like to watch some afternoon serials, but without the sound. She takes an interest in how the people dress and what the furniture in the homes looks like. The actors and actresses are company of sorts when Mr. Garcia is outside tending the crops or looking after the horses and cows. Nor is language the problem; they both prefer to speak Spanish, but they can make themselves understood quite well in English. They have had to, as Mrs. Garcia explains, with no effort to conceal her longstanding sense of resignation: "You bend with the wind. And Anglo people are a strong wind. They want their own way; they can be like a tornado, out to pass over everyone as they go somewhere. I don't mean to talk out of turn. There are Anglos who don't fit my words. But we are outsiders in a land that is ours. We are part of an Anglo country and that will not change. I had to teach the facts of life to my four sons, and in doing so I learned my own lesson well."

She stops and looks at the pictures of her sons that stand on top of the television set. Holding those pictures is an important function of the set, which was given her and her husband by their oldest son. Like his father he is named Domingo, but unlike his father he attended, though he did not finish, high school, in Española, on good days a ride of twenty or so minutes from the Garcias' home. Mrs. Garcia loves to talk about him: "I am a mother. You will forgive me if I am proud; sometimes I know I have been boastful, and I tell the confessor my sin. Domingo was a smart child. He walked quickly. He talked very well from the start. He did good work in school. We would take a walk, and he would point something out to me; often I had never noticed it before. Before he'd entered school he told me he wanted to become a priest. I asked him why. He said because he'd like to know all the secrets of God. It was my fault, of course. He would ask me questions (those endless why's all children ask—I later learned, after I had my second and third and fourth sons) and I would be puzzled, and not know what to answer. So, I would say the same thing my mother used to say to us: that is one of God's secrets. She died when she was ninety, and well before that my little Domingo had asked her when she would die. I lowered my head in shame, as I was taught to do when I was a girl, as I brought up my children to do, as thank God, my grandchildren now do. But my mother smiled and said, 'That is one of God's secrets.' After that, I think, I started to copy her words with my boy Domingo—though memory becomes moldy after a while and falls into pieces, like the cheese I make.

"I am taking you through side streets. I am sorry. Maybe we never know our own confusion; maybe it takes another to help us see what we have come to. I wanted to tell you about Domingo's teachers. They were Anglos. Today some of our own people teach in the schools, but not that many. Domingo was called brilliant by his teachers. They called me in. They said he was the only child in his class who was bright, and who belonged, really belonged in school. They made me listen to their trials with the other children they taught. I was young then, and obedient. I listened. Maybe now I would ask them please to excuse me, but

I have to go home: the bread to make, you know, before supper. But my husband says no, even this very year we still would stay and nod our heads. Can you dare turn away from your child's teacher, just to satisfy your own anger? Our young people, our college students, say yes; but they live far away, under different conditions, not these here.

"The teachers never mentioned college to me. They weren't *that* hopeful about Domingo. I don't think they even thought about a person like us going to college. He just might be worthy of high school, I was told. She had never before said that to one of our children, I was told. He is an exceptional boy, I was told. How did it come about, I was asked. Well, of course, I smiled and said I didn't know. She asked about Domingo's father: was he smarter than the others? I said no, none of us are 'smart,' just trying to get by from day to day, and it's a struggle. That was a bad time, 1930 and the years right after it. Weeks would go by and we would see no money. (We still see little.) And I had already lost four children: the last two had been born in good health, but they died of pneumonia, one at age two, one at age three. You can put yourself in my shoes, I hope. Then, if you will just carry yourself back in time and imagine how hard it was for us, and how little we knew, you will see that I had no way of answering that teacher. On the way home I asked myself, *is* young Domingo 'smart'? Is his father 'smart'? I was afraid to ask his father that evening. He was so tired, so fearful we'd lose even the land under us. He said he'd die and kill us, the child and me, before we went to a city and became lost. When I heard him speaking like that, I forgot the teacher and her question. I served him my bread, and he felt better. Reassured, that is the word."

She stops and serves bread. She pours coffee. It is

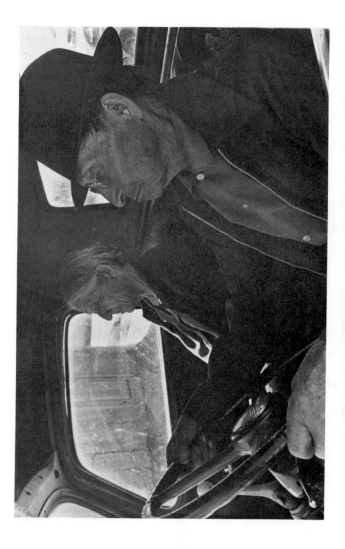

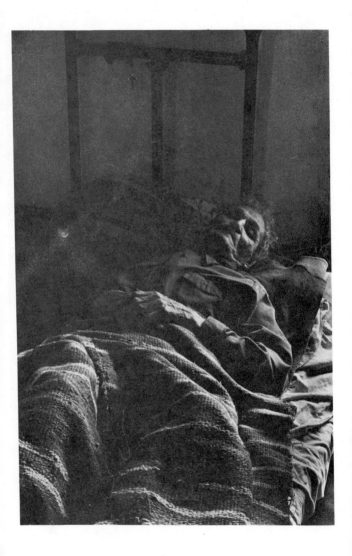

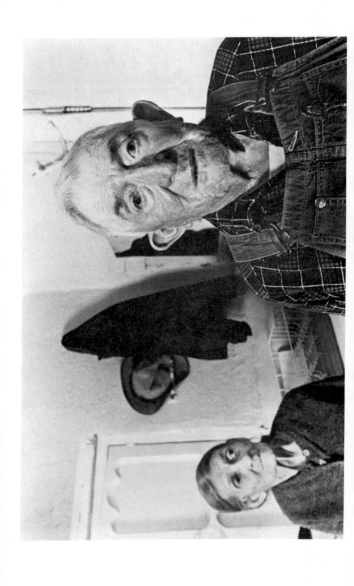

best black, she says in a matter of fact way, but the visitor will not be judged for his weak stomach or poor taste. She again apologizes for her failure to tell a brief, pointed, coherent story. Her mother was "sunny," was "very sunny" until the end, but she worries about "clouds" over her own thinking. The two Domingos in her life scoff at the idea, though. After the coffee she wants to go on. She likens herself to a weathered old tree that stands just outside, within sight. It is autumn and the tree is bare. She likens the coffee to a God-given miracle: suddenly one feels as if spring has come, one is budding and ready to go through another round of things. But she is definitely short of breath, coffee or no coffee, and needs no one to point it out. "Tomorrow then."

In the morning she is far stronger and quicker to speak out than later in the day. "Every day is like a lifetime," she says—immediately disavowing ownership of the thought. Her husband has said that for years, and to be honest, she has upon occasion taken issue with him. Some days start out bad, and only in the afternoon does she feel in reasonably good spirits. But she does get up at five every morning, and most often she is at her best when the first light appears. By the time her visitor arrives, early in the morning by his standards, she has done enough to feel a little tired and somewhat nostalgic: "Each day for me is a gift. My mother taught us to take nothing for granted. We would complain, or beg, as children do before they fall asleep, and she would remind us that if we are *really* lucky we will have a gift presented to us in the morning: a whole new day to spend and try to do something with. I suppose we should ask for more than that, but it's too late for me to do so.

"I prefer to sit here on my chair with my eyes on the mountains. I prefer to think about how the animals

25

are doing; many of them have put themselves to sleep until spring. God has given them senses, and they use them. Things are not so clear for us—so many pushes and pulls, so many voices; I know what Babel means. I go in town shopping and there is so much argument: everyone has an opinion on something. The only time people lower their heads these days is on Sunday morning, for an hour, and even then they are turning around and paying attention to others. What is she wearing? How is he doing with his business? Do we any longer care what the Lord wants us to know and do?

"I am sorry. I am like a sheep who disobeys and has to be given a prod. I don't lose my thoughts when they're crossing my mind; it's when they have to come out as words that I find trouble. We should be careful with our thoughts, as we are with the water. When I'm up and making breakfast I watch for changes in the light. Long before the sun appears it has fore-warned us. Nearer and nearer it comes, but not so gradually that you don't notice. It's like one electric light going on after another. First there is dark. Then the dark lifts ever so little. Still, it might be a full moon and midnight. Then, like Domingo's knife with chick-ens, the night is cut up; it becomes a shadow of what it was, and Domingo will sometimes stop for a minute and say: 'Dolores, she is gone, but do not worry, she will be back.' He has memories like mine: his mother lived to be eighty-seven, and all her life she spoke like mine: 'Domingo, be glad,' she would tell him. Why should he be glad? His mother knew: 'God has chosen you for a trial here, so acquit yourself well every day, and never mind about yesterday or tomorrow.' We both forget her words, though. As the sun comes out of hiding and there is no longer any question that those clouds will go away, we thank dear God for his generosity, but we think back sometimes. We can't seem to help ourselves. We hold on and try to keep in mind the chores that await us, but we are tempted, and soon we will be slipping. There is a pole in our fire station. Once the men are on it, there is no stopping. Like them with a crash we land on those sad moments. We feel sorry for ourselves. We wish life had treated us more kindly. The firemen have a job to do, and I wonder what would happen to us if we didn't have ours to do. We might never come back to this year of 1972. We would be the captives of bad memories. But no worry; we are part of this world here; the sun gets stronger and burns our consciences; the animals make themselves known; on a rainy day the noise of the water coming down the side of the house calls to me— why am I not moving, too?"

She moves rather quickly, so quickly that she seems almost ashamed when someone takes notice, even if silently. Back in her seat she folds her arms, then unfolds them, putting her hands on her lap, her left hand over her right hand. Intermittently she breaks her position to reach for her coffee and her bread: "Domingo and I have been having this same breakfast for over fifty years. We are soon to be married fifty-five years, God willing. We were married a month after the Great War ended; it was a week before Christmas, 1918. The priest said he hoped our children would always have enough food and never fight in a war. I haven't had a great variety of food to give my family, but they have not minded. I used to serve the children eggs in the morning, but Domingo and I have stayed with hot bread and coffee. My fingers would die if they didn't have the dough to work over. I will never give up my oven for a new one. It has been here forty years, and is an old friend. I would stop baking bread if it gave out. My sons once offered to buy me an electric range, they called it, and I broke down. It was a terrible thing to do. The boys felt bad. My husband said I should be more considerate. I meant no harm, though. I didn't deliberately say to myself: Dolores Garcia, you have been hurt, so now go and cry. The tears came and I was helpless before them. Later my husband said they all agreed I was in the right; the stove has been so good to us, and there is nothing wrong—the bread is as tasty as ever, I believe. It is a sickness, you know: being always dissatisfied with what you have, and eager for a change."

She stops here and looks lovingly around the room. She is attached to every piece of furniture. Her husband made them: a round table, eight chairs, with four more in their bedroom, the beds there, the bureau there. She begins to tell how good Domingo is at carving wood: "That is what I would like to say about Domingo: he plants, builds, and harvests, he tries to keep us alive and comfortable with his hands. We sit on what he has made, eat what he has grown, sleep on what he has put together. We have never had a spring on our bed, but I have to admit, we bought our mattress. Buying, that is the sickness. I have gone to the city and watched people. They are hungry, but nothing satisfies their hunger. They come to stores like flies to sticky paper: they are caught. I often wonder who is better off. The fly dies. The people have to pay to get out of the store, but soon they are back again, the same look in their eyes. I don't ask people to live on farms and make chairs and tables; but when I see them buying things they don't need, or even want— except to make a purchase, to get something—then I say there is a sickness.

"I talked to the priest about this. He said yes, he knows. But then he shrugged his shoulders. I knew what he was thinking: the Devil is everywhere, and not until Judgment Day will we be free of him. I watch my son Domingo and his son Domingo; they both have plans: next year we buy this, and the year after, that. Such plans are sad to hear. I try to tell them, but they do not listen. Those are the moments when I feel suddenly old, the only time I do. I turn to the priest. He says I am sinning: my pride makes me think I can disagree with the way the whole country works. I reply, 'No, father, just what I hear my own son and grandson saying.' Hasn't a mother got the right to tell her own flesh and blood that they are becoming slaves —that is it, slaves of habits and desires that have nothing to do with living a good life?"

She sighs and stops talking. She breaks her bread up into small pieces and eats them one by one. She stirs her coffee with a stick her husband made especially for that purpose: it is about six inches long, smoothed out and painted green. He jokes with her: one day she will decide to add milk to her coffee, because her stomach will demand it, and she will comply. Then she will really need the stick. But she has never used milk. Eventually she puts the stick down and resumes: "I am not a priest. I read the Bible, go to church, make my confession, and know I will soon need to come back to tell more. But a good life is a life that is obedient to God's rules, and a life that is your own, not someone else's. God and God alone owns us; it is not right that others own us. There are many kinds of slavery. My children would come home from school and tell me that they were glad they were not colored, because colored people once were slaves. 'Watch out,' I'd say. Their father would agree: you can become a slave without even knowing it. You can be white and have money, but not own your soul. I remember years ago I took the children to town; they were young and they wanted to see Santa Claus. He would come once and only once—and it turned out we missed him. Next year, I told the boys. They pouted. They beseeched me. They wanted me to take them somewhere, anywhere—so long as they could catch sight of Santa Claus. I held my ground. They would not stop. I said no is no. They said please. Finally I had to go after them. I talked as if I was giving a sermon in church. Maybe I ought not have spent so much of their time and mine, but I had to tell them, once and for all, that we have our land, and we feed ourselves and live the best lives we know how to, and we must never feel empty and worthless because of a Santa, or because a salesman has beckoned us, and we have said No, I haven't the money.

"Later I wondered whether I'd done the right thing. I told my husband that Santa Claus is different. Children love him, and why not try very hard to take them to see him? He thought for a while. When he thinks he takes up his pipe and uses it more than he usually does. With each puff I say to myself: there goes one of his thoughts—and I wonder when he'll share them with me. Soon he does, though. It never fails: he puts his pipe down, and then I know I'm to get ready, and pay attention. I sit down and soon I hear. He always starts with: 'My wife, let me tell you what I think.' Soon I know what he thinks, because he's not one to hide behind pretty phrases. As for Santa Claus, Domingo told me what he thought of him: very little. I will never forget his words. He said that Santa Claus has been captured by the storekeepers. He said that they have him locked up, and he will never be free until we stop turning Christmas into a carnival, a time when people become drunk on their greed and take to stores in order to indulge themselves. Of course, the priest lectures us in the same way. And I know we all can be greedy. I eat too much of my bread, more than

I need. I shouldn't. Sometimes I punish myself: the oven is empty for a day or two—once for a week, after a holiday. That time Domingo couldn't stand it any longer. 'I am starving' he told me—even though I made him cereal and eggs instead. But bread for him is life, and I never stopped so long again. I had made a mistake. A nun said to me, Punishment for a sin can *be* a sin. If you are proud of yourself for doing penance, you are defeated before you start."

She stops to open the window and summon her husband. Maybe *he* should say exactly what he told his boys a long time ago about Santa Claus. But no, it is hopeless; he will not come in until he has finished his work. He is like a clock, so-and-so-many minutes to do one thing, then another. The cows know the difference between him and anyone else. He is quick. They get fast relief. When one of her sons tries to help, or she, or a grandchild, it is no good. The animals are restless, make a lot of noise, and Domingo pleads: leave him his few jobs, then when he goes, sell the animals. As for Santa Claus, forgotten for a moment, the gist of Domingo's speech is given by his wife: "My children, a saint is in chains, locked up somewhere, while all these stores have their impostors. Will you contribute to a saint's suffering? Santa Claus was meant to bring good news: the Lord's birthday is in the morning, so let us all celebrate by showing each other how much love we feel. Instead we say, I want, I want, I want. We say, More, more, more. We say Get this, then the next thing, and then the next. We lose our heads. We lose our souls. And somewhere that saint must be in hiding, may be in jail for all we know. If not, he is suffering. I tell you this not to make you feel bad. It is no one's fault. We are all to blame. Only let us stop. If we stop, others will not, I know.

31

But that will be their sorrow, not ours to share with them."

She is not ready to guarantee every word as his. He is a man of few words, and she readily admits that she tends to carry on. Then, as if to confess something that is not a sin, and so not meant for a priest, yet bothers her, she goes further, admits to talking out loud when no one is around. She is sure her husband doesn't do so, and she envies him his quiet self-assurance, his somewhat impassive temperament: "He is silent not because he has nothing to say. He is silent because he understands the world, and because he knows enough to say to himself: what will words and more words do to make the world any better? I have wished for years that I could be like him, but God makes each of us different. When our son Domingo went to school they began teaching him English. We had learned English ourselves, enough to speak. But we didn't speak it, only Spanish. When Domingo started learning English we decided to speak it more and more at home. The same with the other boys. Often I would rehearse my English by myself. I would learn words and expressions from the priest and from the mayor of the town. He was a cousin, and always doing business with Anglos. I learned to talk to myself in English—to my husband in Spanish, but to myself in English! Once my husband overheard me, and he thought I was delirious. He asked if I had a fever. I said no, none at all. He said I sounded as if I did. I said I was learning to speak English. He said he could speak English—but not to himself. Then he laughed and said, 'Dolores, you have spoken Spanish to yourself, too. I have heard you.' Since then I have been more careful, and I don't believe my husband knows that I still have the habit. I don't talk to teach myself English, though. I talk because my mind fills up with words, and then they spill out. Sometimes I talk with someone I imagine nearby. Sometimes I talk to myself. Sometimes it is in Spanish, sometimes in English."

After all the talk of talk, she has nothing more to say. She has to clean the house. She has to start a soup. She always has soup. As one pot begins to empty, she starts another going. It contains bones and vegetables. Soup, that is all it is called. Then she has to sew. There are clothes to mend, clothes to make. Her eyes aren't what they used to be, but with glasses she can see well enough. And finally, the radio. She prefers radio to television. She listens to music. She listens to the weather forecast and either nods or scoffs. Her sons hear the weather and actually believe what they hear. She knows better. She decides early in the morning what the weather will be like and only wants to know how good those weathermen are, with their gadgets and their reports from God knows what far-off cities. She feels sorry for them: they have a lot to learn. She hopes that one day they will go outside and look at the sky, rather than take their readings. It is one more bit of foolishness we have to live with now: "Years ago there were not these weather reports all the time. We would go out and size up the morning. We could tell. We felt the moisture before it turned to rain. If we had any questions we prayed, then more often than not we had an answer. I don't believe it was God's, either. The priest long ago warned us not to ask Him for favors, and not to expect His Answers for the small favors we want. He is up there; we are down here. Once we are born, it is up to us. We pray to show our faith. If we have faith, we can do what is necessary. Not everything was good in the old days; we used to ask God's help all the time and be disappointed. My mother would pray that her bread came out good. I would pray for rain. I think we have stopped that, Domingo and me."

Now it is time to rest. Several times each day she and her husband do so. It is up to her to call him and she does it in such a way that he knows why. In a matter-of-fact way she speaks his name, and slowly he comes in. It is ten o'clock when they rest first. They lie down for five or ten minutes only, but that does miracles for them. They get up refreshed not only in body but in mind, and, evidently, soul: "I pray. I thank God for the time he has given me here, and ask Him to take me when He is ready, and I tell Him I will have no regrets. I think of all I have seen in this long life: the people, the changes. Even up here, in this small village, the world makes its presence felt. I remember when the skies had no planes in them, houses no wires sticking up, trying to catch television programs. I never wanted a refrigerator. I never needed one. But I have one. It is mostly empty. I have one weakness: ice cream. I make it, just as I make butter. I used to make small amounts and Domingo and I would finish what was there. Now I can make and store up butter or ice cream and give presents of them to my sons and their children. No wonder they bought us the refrigerator! As I lie on our bed and stare at the ceiling I think how wonderful it is: eighty-three, and still able to make ice cream. We need a long rest afterwards, but between the two of us we can do a good job. The man at the store has offered to sell any extra we have; he says he can get a good price. I laugh. I tell him he's going to turn me into a thief. It would be dishonest to sell food you make in your home for profit at a store. That's the way I feel. My husband gets angry: What do you mean 'dishonest?' he will say. I answer back: my idea of what is dishonest is not his. So we cannot go on about this. It is in my heart where the feeling is, not in my head.

'Oh, you are a woman!' he says, and he starts laughing. Later he will tell me that he was picking weeds, or taking care of our flowers, and he thought to himself: She is right, because to make food is part of our life as a family, and to start selling that is to say that we have nothing that is *ours*. It is what he always comes back to: better to have less money and feel we own ourselves, than more and feel at the mercy of so many strangers."

The two of them show a burst of energy after they get up. As they have rested, said their prayers, reminisced, they have given thought to what they will do next, and so, when they are ready, they set out decisively. It is almost as if they know they have limited time, know that soon they will again have to interrupt their working rhythm for lunch and another rest afterwards. "I am a new person several times a day," she points out, then adds right away, "But I can suddenly get quite tired." She feels "weakness" and "a loss of breath" come on, her way of describing the effects of a cardiovascular difficulty common to people in their eighties. Yet she sees no doctor, hasn't seen one in decades: "There are no doctors near here. I would have to go to Española. I would, if there was a need. I have pains all over; it is arthritis, I know. One can't expect joints to hold up forever. I do not believe in aspirin. I do not believe in medicines. I have to pant like our dog when I move too fast for too long. I have to stop and catch up. It is the lungs and the heart, I know. My son wants me to go get a checkup. My ankles swell at the end of the day, but the next morning they are down again. The body has its seasons. I am in the last one; winter is never without pain and breakdowns. I don't want to spend my last years waiting on myself and worrying about myself. I have already lived over twice as long as our Savior. How greedy ought one be for life? God has his purposes. I wake up and feel those aches and I notice how wrinkled my skin is, and I wonder what I'm still doing alive. I believe it is wrong, to ask a question like that. One lives. One dies. To ask questions with no good answers to them is to waste time that belongs to others. I am here to care for my husband, to care for this house, to be here when my sons and my grandchildren come. The young have to see what is ahead. They have to know that there is youth and middle age and old age. My grandson Domingo asked me a while ago what it is like to be one hundred. He is ten. I told him to be one hundred is to live ten of his lifetimes. He seemed puzzled, so I knew I had been thoughtless. I took him around. I put my hand beside his and we compared skins. I said it is good to be young and it is good to be old. He didn't need any more explanations. He said when you're young you have a lot of years before you, but when you're old you have your children and your grandchildren and you love them and you're proud of them. I took him around again and hugged him tightly, and in a second he was out there with his father and his grandfather looking at the cows."

She doesn't spend too much time with the cows, but the chickens are hers to feed and look after. She cleans up their fenced-in enclosure, and delights in their eggs. She and her husband have one hard-boiled egg each for lunch every day. She gives her sons eggs regularly; a nephew and niece also get some. She feeds the chickens leftovers, and some of her fresh bread as well. She is convinced that they lay better eggs because of her bread. One day for the sake of a visitor she borrowed a store-bought egg and compared it with one of hers: each was dropped in hot water for poaching, and hers did indeed stay much more intact and turn out tastier. "Animals today are turned into machines," she remarked after the experiment. She shook her head. She tried not to be gloomy, but she was worried: "No one my age has the right to demand that the world stand still. So much was wrong in the past that is better now. I didn't want this refrigerator, but it is good to have, now that I'm used to it. My grandchildren have had narrow misses with death, but doctors have saved them. I still mourn the babies I lost. Even if I'd been rich back then I might have lost them. Now there are medicines to kill the bad germs. But to see chickens or cows being kept in one place and stuffed with food that isn't really food—Domingo says they are fed chemicals —so they will grow fat all of a sudden, and have their eggs or become fit for slaughter: that is unnatural. I ask myself: Did God form the beasts of the field, and the fowl of the air so that they should be treated this way by man? I asked the priest once, and he scratched his head and said he would have to think about it. The next time I saw him I looked at him hard and he remembered my question. 'Mrs. Garcia, you don't make it easy for me,' he said. I smiled and said I didn't want to cause any trouble, but I can't help thinking about some of these things. He answered. 'I don't know what to say.' Then I decided I'd best not trouble him any more. He once told me that a priest only knows what Christ promised us; how He will bring about His promises—that's not for man to know. I thought afterwards I ought to confess to him my boldness—the sin of pride. Who am I to decide they have no right to run those chicken farms? But God forgive me, I still believe it is wrong: I still believe animals ought not to be turned into machines."

She arranges the eggs she brings in very carefully; she takes them out of her basket and puts them in a bowl. Some are brown, some white. She likes to fix them up like flowers; they give a freckled appearance from afar. When she uses some, she rearranges those

37

that are left. She handles them not only with care but with pride and affection. Sometimes as she talks and does her work with the eggs she will hold a warm one in her hand: "I feel comforted by a fresh egg. It is sad to feel it get colder, but that is life. My granddaughter loves to help me collect eggs. The other day she asked me if the eggs inside a woman are the same kind as those that come out of a chicken. I was taken aback. I told her I didn't think so. Then I wondered what else to say. My husband said later there isn't anything more to say. The priest agreed. I felt I'd failed the little girl, though: I changed subjects on her before she even knew what had happened. A few minutes later I could tell her mind was back with the eggs, and she wanted to ask me more questions. But I wouldn't let her. I didn't tell her no, at least not directly. I just kept up my line of chatter. The poor girl, she was overcome by her grandmother's words—and by her own shyness! This time I didn't go to the priest later and ask him what I should have said. I have never talked to him about such matters. When one is young they are too personal; and besides, what is there to ask, and what is there to say? Also, a priest is entitled to respect: they are not living a worldly life, and there is much they don't know. I think our new priest is like a youth, even if he is fifty; I mean, he has never tasted of life. That is what a priest is about, of course; his passions go up toward the altar, and then to Heaven. So, I sat and thought about how to talk with my granddaughter the next time. I hope I can do her some justice. Time will tell. One never knows what to say except when the moment is at hand. I do rehearse conversations sometimes, though, I have to admit."

She stops abruptly, as if this is one conversation she doesn't want to pursue. Anyway, she has been dusting and sweeping the floor as she talks and now she is finished. Next come the plants, a dozen or so of them; they need to be watered and moved in or out of the sun. She hovers over them for a minute, doing nothing, simply looking. She dusts them, too. She prunes one: "I've been waiting for a week or so to do this. I thought to myself: that plant won't like it, losing so much. I dread cutting my toenails and fingernails. I am shaky with scissors. But I go after the plants with a surer touch. They are so helpless, yet they are so good to look at. They seem to live forever. Parts die, but new parts grow. I have had them so long—I don't remember the number of years. I know each one's needs, and I try to take care of them the same time each day. Maybe it is unnecessary nonsense, the amount of attention I give. I know that is what Domingo would say. Only once did he put his belief into words, and then I reminded him that he has his habits, too. No one can keep him from starting in one corner of his garden and working his way to the other, and with such care. I asked him years ago why not change around every once in a while and begin on the furthest side, and go faster. 'I couldn't do it,' he said, and I told him I understood. Habits are not crutches; habits are roads we have paved for ourselves. When we are old, and if we have done a good job, the roads last and make the remaining time useful: we get where we want to go, and without the delays we used to have when we were young. How many plants died on me when I was first learning! How often I forgot to water them, or watered them too much because I wanted to do right. Or I would expose them to the sun and forget that, like us, they need the shade, too. I was treating them as if they needed a dose of this, a trial of that. But they have been removed from God's forests, from Nature it is; and they need consideration. When we were young my husband also used to forget chores; he'd be busy doing

39

one thing, and he'd overlook the other. But slowly we built up our habits, and now I guess we are protected from another kind of forgetfulness: the head tires easily when you are our age, and without the habits of the years you can find yourself at a loss to answer the question: what next?"

She turns to lunch. She stirs the soup. She warms up the bread. She reaches for the eggs. She sets a simple, careful table, a large spoon and a knife for herself, her husband, and their guest. Each gets a napkin from a set given her half a century ago by her mother, and used on Sundays, holidays, special occasions. She is apologetic: "I fear we often look at these napkins but don't use them. No wonder they survive so well! They remind us to behave ourselves, because it is no ordinary day; and so, we eat more carefully, and don't have to use them. They are usually in the same condition when I put them away as when I took them out. My grandmother made them, gave them to my mother, and now I have them. My three daughters died as infants; I will give the napkins to my eldest son's wife. I tried to do so when they were married, but she said no. I insisted, and only got more refusals. If she had been my daughter, she would have accepted. But I was not hurt. It takes time to move over from one family and be part of another. She would accept the napkins now, but they would become frightened if suddenly I offered them. Is she sick? Does she know something we don't know? What have we done to neglect her, that she offers us what she loves to put on her own table? So, I will have them until the end, when all possessions obtain new masters."

She has to go outside. It is cold and windy, but sunny. There is some fresh milk there in a pail—from cows which, she hastens to add, present no danger of sickness to a visitor who up until that moment had taken

40

for granted the word *pasteurized* that appears on every milk bottle or carton. And she has herself and her husband as proof—a touch of reassurance which she obviously enjoys being able to offer: "My sons' wives sometimes hesitate, too. I can see what they think on their faces. They deny it, but I know: Is it safe to drink milk right from the cow? They are from the city, and they have no way of understanding that many cows are quite healthy; their owners know when they are sick. Anyway, Domingo and I survived without store milk, and we are not young, and not so sick we can't work or eat—or drink milk."

She wraps herself in a sweater she has made and upon opening the door quickly turns back for a moment: "Oh, the wind." But she persists, and is gone. When she is back, she resumes where she has left off: "The wind can be a friend or an enemy. A severe wind reminds us of our failures: something we forgot to fasten down. A gentle wind is company. I have to admit, I can spend a long time listening to the wind go through trees, watching it sweep across the grass. Domingo will come in and say, 'Oh, Dolores, come out and watch the wind go through the grass.' I hurry out. I often wonder if the ground feels it—like hair being combed and brushed. I walk with our dog and he gets scents from far off, carried by the wind. I tell him not to be tricked. Better to let things quiet down, then take another scent. He is over ten, and should not run long distances. He doesn't know his own limits. But who does, exactly? It takes a lifetime to get used to your body, and by the time you do, then it is almost time to say good-bye and go elsewhere. I often wonder whether the wind carries our soul skyward. It is another of my foolish ideas, and I put it to the priest long ago—not this one, but the one who came before him. He was annoyed with me. 'Mrs. Garcia,' he said, 'you have an

41

active imagination.' I apologized. He reminded me that God's ways are not ours. I wanted to tell him that the wind comes mysteriously from above and might be one of many good, strong arms our Lord has. But I knew to keep quiet was best. He was a very stern priest, and outspoken. He would not have hesitated to dress me down severely and warn me publicly that I would pay for that kind of talk in Hell. Once he cuffed my husband because Domingo told him he'd heard that much of our weekly collection was going to Africa or Asia, to places way off, and meanwhile so many people hereabouts are without work and go hungry.

"It was in the bad years, in the 1930s. We were poor, but at least we had our land. Others had nothing. And the priest was fat. He was waited on, and he dined on the best; we were told that by the woman who cooked for him. Mind you, she did not serve him. He had to have someone special to do that. And he paid them a pittance. They had children they were supporting; and, alas, husbands too. In a good mood he would promise them an eternity in Heaven. On bad days he would threaten them with Purgatory and no escape—so, of course, they would leave his kitchen in tears, clutching their rosary beads all the way home. My husband heard of this, and was enraged. He said terrible things. I pleaded with him to stop. We were so poor, and the bank threatened to take away our small farm. Some people had thought of marching on the bank. The bank officials heard of the plan and never made a move against us. By then I had lost four children. I will not repeat what Domingo said about the priest—or the Church. The worse his language, the harder I prayed. I kneeled by my bed and prayed one evening after he had carried on a full hour, it seemed; it must have really been a few minutes, I now know, but I thought he would never stop. Then a heavy wind came, later that

42

evening, and I was sure: God was approaching us to exact his punishment. And why not, after Domingo's outburst? He was tidying up outside. He had calmed down. I had heard him say a Hail Mary, but I pretended to be lost in my own work. He didn't want me to know that he had taken back the words he had spoken; he is proud. I decided to pray for him, but I was sure something bad would happen. Nothing did, though; the wind came, then left. A week afterwards I told Domingo of my fears. He laughed and said we are too intelligent, both of us, even without education, to be superstitious. I agreed. But a month later he came in one day for lunch and he told me he had to confess something to me. I said, Not to me, to the priest. No, he had very little to tell that priest, only the briefest of admissions once a month. I said nothing. He said that he'd been afraid too, that evening after he'd lost his temper. When the wind came, and he was outside, and the horses started whinnying and the dog ran back and forth, he did not know what to do or why the animals were upset; so he had gotten down on his knees and asked God's forgiveness. He'd even asked Him to take us both, with the house: through a tornado, perhaps. But soon it became very still, and I think each of us must have been holding our breaths, without knowing we were doing so together, like so much else we do! I fear that when he goes, I will, or when I go, he will. But I have no right to such thoughts: it is not up to me or to Domingo, but to our Lord and Savior. We are sinners, though, and we can't help being selfish. There will be no future for either of us alone. I only hope we are not tested by being separated for too long by death!"

When her husband comes in, without being called, she says that it is now noon. They go by the sun. They have a clock in their bedroom, but they rarely use it. They forget to wind it, except when their son is coming and they want to show him that they like his present: "Domingo gave us the clock, and I treasure it. I look at it and think of him. We only have two sons. It is nice to be reminded of them. I don't mean to sound as if I pity myself. Our son Domingo works at Los Alamos. He says it is maintenance he does; he looks after all those scientists. They leave their laboratories in a mess, and someone has to pick up after them, or everything would stop cold one day. He gets a good wage, and jobs are few around here, so he is lucky to be there. He could have stayed with us, worked on the land. But all we have is our animals and the crops—no money. I put up many jars for the winter, but jars of food are not enough to attract young people, and I see their view. There are a hundred like Domingo who would like his job. Before they brought in the laboratories at Los Alamos, there was nothing anywhere near here. Domingo would be in Albuquerque, I believe, if it hadn't been for Los Alamos. My younger son is down there. I've never even been to Santa Fe. He drives up here on weekends. His life is difficult, living in the city. I don't ask him much; I wouldn't understand. His wife longs to come back here. He does, too. But how can they? No work. Domingo was interviewed several times for his job. He took a test, I believe. He did well. The teachers who predicted good for him, they were right. It's too bad he didn't finish high school; the war came, the one against Japan and Hitler.

"Then came the next war. My second son, Francisco, went to Korea. He was there for many months. I remember well the Saturday morning that I got news of him. I remember the day he came home. I was sitting in this very chair. I had to mend some of my husband's clothes. I was almost through, and as it does, my mind was already preparing for the next step in the day: a visit outside to pick some tomatoes. Suddenly the door opened, with no warning. Who could it be—the front door, hardly ever used, rather than the side one right here? My boy Domingo—he lived with us then, and worked as a handyman in the school where they had always thought so well of him. He had his suit on. 'Domingo,' I said, 'why the suit?' He did not answer. For a second I wondered how he had slipped in and put it on without my knowing. We will do anything not to see what is right before us. I believe I might have wondered and wondered about such petty questions—but after Domingo came his father, also with a suit on. I got up and shouted, 'It is not Sunday!' I said it over and over again. 'It is not, it is not!' Then I started crying. They never told me. I never asked. I just knew. My husband asked me if I wanted to change my dress. I said no. I am a plain woman, and my son was a plain man—no pretenses. He did not die in his Sunday clothes. They turned around and I followed them. We walked down that road, two miles. I saw nothing. I heard nothing. I was alone, even though they were with me, one on each side. Once I must have looked near collapse. I felt their hands and was surprised to see them standing there. Then I dropped my beads. I picked them up, but I didn't say the Rosary. I just kept holding onto the beads. They had brought the body to the basement of the school building, a United States flag around it. Later, after the funeral, they wanted to give me that flag; I said no, it could stay at the school. Let the children see what war means. That is something they should learn—as much as how to read and write and count. It is no good when flags are used that way."

She has gone too far to suit her sense of propriety. She insists upon her ignorance. Who is she to talk about wars? They come about through events she has no knowledge of. She has a place in God's scheme of things; best to stay in it. But something makes her rest-

45

less, no matter how she tries to put aside her doubts and misgivings. She stands up, walks toward her plants, and examines them, one by one. They are all right. She goes back to her chair. Then she is up offering coffee, serving a delicious chocolate marble cake she has made —from a packaged mix, a concession on her part to her daughter-in-law's urging. Once again seated, she interrupts a conversation about the "new road"—the road in front of her house which now for the first time is paved—to put into words what she can't stop thinking about: "There was another time. Two years ago, before that road was fixed up to be so strong it can ignore the weather, I had walked down to talk with my neighbor. She had suffered badly from pneumonia, but was on the mend. As I came toward the house I saw them again. You know, this time I thought my mind had left me. I wiped my eyes, but they wouldn't go away. I called to them, but they didn't answer, so I was sure they weren't there. It was late afternoon, a time when shadows begin to appear, and one can be fooled, anyway. So I wiped my eyes again, and when they remained, I looked around, hoping to see them in back of me, too. Then I would know; my eyes, my head—something for a doctor to heal, or a warning from God that it won't be long. Well, soon they were upon me; it was only when I *felt* them that I believed they were there and I was there. I remember thinking that perhaps I'd fallen asleep at my neighbor's, or maybe I'd taken a nap at my own house and now was waking up. In a second one can have such thoughts. In another second one can know everything without hearing a word. I said, 'How did it happen?' My husband couldn't talk. I held on to him and wanted him to tell me, but he was speechless. My son tried to tell me, but he couldn't finish his story. He used the word 'car,' and that was enough for me. Later they tried to give me the details,

46

and I begged them to stop. Those suits on a day in the middle of the week! There have been days since when I have wanted to burn those suits or tear them to shreds. There have been days when I have lost all faith. I dared not go to confession; I could not let a priest hear what was on my mind. I cringed before God, knowing He hears everything, even what is not spoken but crosses the mind, a rabbit of an idea, suddenly upon you, quickly chased away, but back again in an unsuspecting moment, when all is quiet."

With that she stopped talking and looks out the window. What ought a visitor do—sit still and wait or find an excuse to leave immediately? Suddenly, though, she is talking again, a bit more softly and slowly and reflectively, but with no apparent distress. And she seems to want to talk: "The mountains, our mountains—I look at them when I need an anchor. They are here. They never leave us. Birds come, stay a while, leave. The moon is here, then gone. Even the sun hides from us for days on end. Leaves don't last, nor flowers. We have had a number of dogs, and I remember them in my prayers. But those mountains are *here*. They are nearer God than us; sometimes I imagine Him up there, on top of one or another mountain, standing over us, getting an idea how we're doing. It is wrong to think like that, I know. But a poor old woman like me can be allowed her foolishness. Who is without a foolish hope? Who doesn't make up dreams to fit his wishes? Sometimes I walk up toward the mountains. I can't go as far now as before. I don't tell my husband I'm going; he would worry that I'd lose my breath completely and no one would be around. But I pace myself, and, as I say, I have to be content with approaching those hills.

"The other day I walked toward them and there was a meeting on the side of the road. I stopped and

47

listened. I never went any further. They were our young men, and some people from the city. *Chicanos,* they spoke of Chicanos. We are Chicanos; nothing else will do, they said. I came home and told my husband. Yes, he said, we are Chicanos. We are so many things, he said. 'Mexican American,' 'Mexicano,' they'd call my boys at school, those Anglo teachers. I would say nothing. They thought then it was their right to call us what they pleased. Spanish, we are Spanish. Many of us may have some Indian blood, too. But I will tell you: I am a woman and a mother and Domingo a man and a father, and both of us belong to this country and no other, and we owe allegiance to the state of New Mexico. Should we give ourselves one name or another, or should we get each day's job done? I can't believe Christ wants us to be Anglo against Chicano, or Chicano against Anglo; but the world is full of bitterness, and when will there be an end to it, *when?* I wondered while I walked home. It is a bad thing to say, but I was glad to come upon that meeting; it took my mind off myself and my memories. I saw that others want to know why there is so much injustice in the world. For a few days after my son was killed in the accident I wondered again whether God cared. I know He is there, watching over us; but I would wake up in the night and my forehead would be wet and I would be shaking. I had dreamed that God had fallen asleep, and so we all were going to suffer: the Devil would win his fight. I thought of those days, now gone, while I listened to the young people shouting 'Chicano!' They mentioned all the bad, nothing good; Domingo says that is how it goes when people have been hurt, and I nodded, because I remembered how I once felt."

One morning, in the midst of a conversation, she scolds herself for talking too much. She falls silent. She glances up at the picture of Christ at the Last

Supper. Her face loses its tension. She slumps a bit, but not under the weight of pain or even age. She feels relaxed. There are a few dishes to wash. There is a curtain that needs mending. There is not only bread to make, but pies. Her grandchildren love her pies, and she loves seeing them eaten. "Children eat so fast," she says with a sigh of envy. She begins talking again. She resumes her activity. She has to pick at her food now. "When one is over eighty the body needs less," she observes—but immediately afterwards she looks a little shy, a little apprehensive: "I have no business talking like a doctor. Once the priest told me I talk like him. I told him: I have raised children; it is necessary at times to give them sermons, and hear their confessions. He smiled. If I had another life I would learn to be a nurse. In my day, few of our people could aim so high—not a woman like me, anyway. It is different today. My sons say their children will finish high school and my Domingo in Los Alamos says *his* Domingo does so well in school he may go on to a college. I laugh with my husband: a Domingo Garcia in a college. Maybe the boy will be a doctor. Who knows? He likes to take care of his dog. He has a gentle side to him. He is popular with the girls, so I don't think he's headed for the priesthood. He tells me he'd like to be a scientist, like the men his father looks after in the laboratories. I worry that he would make those bombs, though. I wouldn't want that on his conscience. My son told me they do other things there in the laboratories, not just make bombs. I said, 'Thank God!'

"Of course all of that is for the future. I don't know if I will be around to see my grandchildren have children of their own. One cannot take anything for granted. The priest laughed at Domingo and me last Sunday, and said, 'You two will outlast me; you will be coming here when you are both over one hundred.' I said, 'Thank you father, but that is a long way off, to be a hundred, and much can happen.' 'Have faith,' he said, and he is right: one must."

She pauses for a few seconds, as if to think about her own admonition. Then she is back on her train of thought: "Sometimes after church Domingo and I walk through the cemetery. It is a lovely place, small and familiar. We pay our respects to our parents, to our aunts and uncles, to our children. A family is a river; some of it has passed on and more is to come, and nothing is still, because we all move along, day by day, toward our destination. We both feel joy in our hearts when we kneel on the grass before the stones and say a prayer. At the edge of the cemetery near the gate is a statue of the Virgin Mary, larger than all the other stones. She is kneeling and on her shoulder is the Cross. She is carrying it—the burden of her Son's death. She is sad, but she has not given up. We know that she has never lost faith. It is a lesson to keep in mind. We always leave a little heavy at the sight of our Lord's mother under such a heavy obligation. But my husband never fails to hold my arm, and each Sunday his words are the same: 'Dolores, the Virgin will be an example to us this week.' It is as if each Sunday he is taking his vows—and me, too, because I say back to him, 'Yes, Domingo, she will be an example to us.' Now, mind you, an hour later one of us, or both of us, will have stumbled. I become cranky. Domingo has a temper. I hush him, and he explodes. He is inconsiderate, and I sulk. That is the way with two people who have lived together so long: the good and the bad are always there, and they have become part of one life, lived together."

She hears his footsteps coming and quickens her activity a bit. She will not be rushed, but he needs his coffee and so does she. Often she doesn't so much need it as need to drink it because he is drinking it. He lifts his cup, she follows; he puts his down, and soon enough hers is also on the table. Always they get through at the same time. This particular morning Domingo is more expansive and concerned than usual —a foal has just been born. "Well, enough. I must go check on the mother and her infant." He is up and near the door when he turns around to say goodbye: "These days one never knows when the end will come. I know our time is soon up But when I look at that mother horse and her child in the barn, or at my children and their children, I feel lucky to have been permitted for a while to be part of all this life here on earth." His hand is on the door, and he seems a little embarrassed to have spoken so. But he has to go on: "I am talking like my wife now! After all these years she sometimes falls into my silences and I carry on as she does. She is not just an old woman, you know. She wears old age like a bunch of fresh-cut flowers. She is old, advanced in years, *vieja,* but in Spanish we have another word for her, a word which tells you that she has grown with all those years. I think that is something one ought hope for and pray for and work for all during life: to grow, to become not only older but a bigger person. She is old, all right, *vieja,* but I will dare say this in front of her: she is *una anciana;* with that I declare my respect and have to hurry back to the barn."

# 3

# LA NECESIDAD

It is a miracle, she believes, that he still requires frequent haircuts at seventy-nine. Her own father was bald by forty, and her sons have tended toward baldness in early middle age. But in another year, she points out, he will be "twenty years short of a hundred," and yet his hair is as thick and bushy as it was years ago—and mostly black, too. Perhaps he is lucky in his ancestry, or perhaps it has to do with the care she has given him all these years. As for him, he mentions the alternatives, but inclines to the latter explanation: "There is a picture of my grandfather; it was taken in Albuquerque a long time ago, perhaps when this century was beginning its life. I must have been six or seven. I remember my father pointing to his father and saying 'My boy, there is someone for both of us to look up to. He will die a strong man, however old he is when God calls him. And look at his hair: as full and black as it was a long time ago.' I asked why people get white hair or lose their hair, and my father shrugged his shoulders: that is up to God.

"I do not mean to speak out of turn, but I believe my wife has been the one responsible for my condition. She has taken such good care of me; she keeps her eye on me as though she were my patron saint. She is more than a good woman whom I married and have loved all these years. She is like a watchdog. She would not mind the comparison. She senses something bad approaching well before it gets near, and she knows how to take a stand: Manuel, I don't like this, or Manuel, let us beware—that is what I hear from her. So, then I know; and I do as she suggests.

"As for my hair, she has cut it every month or so for over half a century. The storekeeper tells me that hair runs in the family: father to son. I tell him no! Look at my sons! He scratches his head; he can't answer me. But I can explain things to him: the boys went into the army, and when they came back they did not want their mother to cut their hair. And that was that! They began losing their hair."

He puts his right hand through his hair. He suddenly feels shy and tries to change the subject: there is a wind coming up, and it will go through the canyon fast. But his mind is still on his hair. Embarrassed by his own pride, he tries again to call upon the weather: Why are New Mexico's winters these days so wet and cold? It has always been cold up in the Sandia mountains, east of Albuquerque; he knows that. But lately there have been extremes—more snow, lower temperatures, noisier and more forceful winds. As he mentions all that he edges closer to the mirror, the one mirror in his house; it hangs on the living room wall rather than in a bedroom or bathroom. For a second he tries to stop himself, but it is no use: better to let oneself go, submit to the pull upon him, and then make a public acknowledgement of what happened: "Mirrors have magnets in them; I've never seen one, but you know a magnet by its feel. Sometimes I will walk into this room, and the next thing I know, I am looking at myself. I don't know why. Maybe it is because I am soon to go, and one wants to say good-bye to an old friend. My mother used to say to us 'Be your own friend; be friendly to others, but don't forget yourself.'

"She did not mean for us to be greedy. She just

wanted us to take care of ourselves. Respect your appearance; she would always give us that advice. I suppose that is why I have not fallen to pieces, even at my age. I am old, but I can still recognize myself—the man I used to be, and soon no longer will be! But I should not speak so much about myself. I should not take such pleasure in my health and my good head of hair. My wife always says that to me: What a good head of hair! And then I am once again overcome by her words: I move toward the mirror to take a look at myself and smile. That is not why we were put here, to pay so much attention to ourselves."

Now he is no longer intent on catching a glimpse of his mostly black hair, nicely combed back. He has been satisfied, and is genuinely anxious to get on with other matters: "I had word from my son today. He called our neighbors. He wants to know why I will never agree to a phone. I try to tell him that I have lived all my life without one, so why begin now? Besides, it costs money. I am not starving, but I am not surrounded by piles of money. We have all we can do to keep our heads high—and only when you owe no one anything can you walk into church and feel you can look to the right or the left, and catch anyone's eye, and not be moved to lower your own eyes right away. I think it bothers my son more to ask a favor—that I be called over to talk with him—than it bothers me to come and speak.

"He is proud. He wants me to be my own master, he tells me. I tell him he is wasting his time: I am too near the end to start learning new tricks. It's not only the money; I think if I was rich I'd feel the same way about the telephone. I have been in homes and heard those phones ring. The church bells are more to my liking. They call you to prayer, but they are polite and not in such a hurry. The phone is like a knife; it lunges at you, then it lunges again: no mercy, no consideration, only determined to make you bow to its wishes. My son laughs; I am at his home and the phone rings, and his wife is out and he is unable to answer, and I know I must be of help, so I say 'I surrender,' and go to pick it up. Later we will be eating and for no reason at all he will look at me and begin to smile. What is on his mind, we all wonder. Finally he tells us: 'Father has one enemy that he cannot banish, but neither will he himself be conquered—the phone. He surrenders when it commands him, but he has his fortress, his own house, and it will never be conquered. It is a stand off." So, we all laugh.

"When you are old, people chalk up everything to your age. You are not entitled to have an opinion without someone saying 'It is because he passed three score and ten that he thinks like that.' My wife will tell our children how stubborn I am; I have had my ideas all my life. But the children, for all the love they have for us, will not listen. They are willing to ignore their own memories. When I try to remind them myself, I receive a smile and a nod: 'Yes, father, anything you say.' I want to stand up and shout, but an old man doesn't shout in his children's home, nor in his own. I would lose my temper years ago; my sons have heard me carry on. But once they left this house to live elsewhere and begin their own families, they returned as guests of mine. As for their mother, she has had a long vacation from my angry outbursts. When one gets older there is not the energy for them."

Perhaps he has given the wrong impression. He worries that he has portrayed himself a spent volcano. He looks for a way of correcting himself. Finally he abandons any need he may have felt for being casual, and instead speaks bluntly: "I no longer have children to discipline. When the boys were younger I would have to teach them how to behave. Their mother would go so far with them; then I had to step in. Six boys, and no girls; I was a father of sons! It would be the same with daughters, though: a father is the one to hand down the laws to children. Of course, there is always disobedience, and I never wanted to crush my young ones. They will never learn if they don't have a chance to go wrong; my wife and I both would say that, especially when we were tempted to go after one of the boys too much. But there is a line one draws, and it is just as well to make it clear; beyond this point—well, there will have to be punishment. I would not use my hands; I have never thought of hitting anyone. I would call them to me, and hold both their hands and look at them. They would lower their eyes, a signal to me that they knew they had done wrong. Then I would tell them what they had to do.

"So, I wasn't harsh. And I always had my father's example to call upon. I am now what he was: a grandfather. In this community a grandfather is respected; he has spent a lot of time bringing up children, making sure they learn to respect their parents, their teachers, their church. He is not put out to pasture when he gets old. He is asked to give advice. I believe my sons really want us to have a phone because it will make it easier for them to ask me questions. Now they have to leave their homes and come here, or wait until I go visit them. If we had a phone, they would just pick it up. But it is better we talk when we can see each other's faces. I tell my oldest son all the time: a voice without a face is like the wind, it comes and is soon gone. I will never forget my father's eyes. I will never forget his large hands, and how they would move toward me when he wanted me to know how serious he was. I remember he would be stern with me, then reach out and hold my upper arm and shake it a little; then I knew I was forgiven and was still loved.

"The other day my third son came to me and we talked about his children. He said they get very noisy sometimes, and their mother's nerves become worn thin. He said he wished I was there all the time, because when I enter the house, the children become like angels; they stop their mischief and look at me as if I was the priest and ready to say benediction—or give a strict sermon. I reminded my son of the mischief he used to cause. I was sitting in this, my chair, and he was over there on the sofa, and I suddenly lowered my voice and told him to come over. He was a little surprised, but he came immediately. Maybe at first he thought I was sick. But when I held his arms as I used to, he knew what I meant: when a father wants to, he can command silence. I used to walk into a room, and the boys would be going after each other, and at first they would not be sure what I was up to, so they would continue. (I never wanted my children to quake in their boots at the very sight of me!) Then I would make myself clear; I would clench my fist and pound the table or if there was no table in the room, I would hit the wall, just once. That was all I needed to do.

"Now it is for me to remind my sons what I used to do, and give them the courage to follow in my footsteps, just as I always turned to my father when I was in doubt about how to be a good example for my children. When he was alive he would show me. He would remind me of his stick. It was in the corner, and when he would be tired of putting up with our foolishness and mistakes, he'd walk over and grab the stick. He never used it. He never even came near us with it. We knew what he wanted. We became different. We stopped our noise and tears and went about our business. Now, I have to admit: I could never use a stick like that. I tried, but I found myself shaking. I had nothing to say, but my throat would catch. I told my wife that a stick was not for me. I talked with my father, and he said he had thrown the stick out after we were all grown, and it was up to me how I taught my children. He said that his father never used a stick; he would stamp his feet hard on the floor. That was all he had to do. I asked my father why he did not do the same. He said he tried, but his feet just wouldn't oblige. All of a sudden they became heavy and he found them more disobedient than us! So, one day he took mother's broom instead. Afterward, he decided he would find a stick for himself: 'It would have been wrong to depend upon your mother's broom,' he told me when I was already a father myself. 'That was for her to use—on the house, not the children!'

"So, you see, we each have to be ourselves. My father had helped me. I came home and thought to myself: why not be like my grandfather? The next day I stamped my feet when two of the boys needed to be told to stop fighting. But it was no good; they missed my point. I pounded on the table, and they heard. From that day on it was my way of being their father. One of my sons does the very same thing. Another takes off his belt and puts it on the table, but he doesn't have to use it. We took a long walk, and he told me his boy was getting fresh. I said that it was better to move quickly against the Devil, and he laughed. He said he wasn't going to pound on the table; and I laughed. I said I could understand. He asked me if I wanted to try pounding the table with my grandchildren. I said they never show me how bad they can be; that is one of the joys of being a grandfather. Well, we walked further, and my son said he would do *something,* and I knew then he would find the answer. When I found out what the answer was I had to laugh:

my great-uncle, my grandfather's older brother, was a great one for the strap. My father said his uncle could take off his strap so fast no one could see him do it; they only heard the snap. Then it was there, on the table. Maybe my son heard me tell the story years ago. We don't forget certain things we hear."

He fusses with his own belt as he talks, then catches himself doing so and gives his visitor a knowing smile. Snow has begun to fall, and he looks at it intently. The weather becomes an occasion for a speech of sorts —about the state of New Mexico, about the region in the state he and his family have considered their home for so long, about the difference between his kind of life and the life Anglo tourists or middle-class suburban people live. He begins, characteristically, with an apology or two. Who is he to speak with any authority? He is scarcely able to read and write. He is merely a working man who at this stage of his life has to be careful not to work very hard. For that reason he sometimes judges himself lazy—and a lazy man, an idle man, ought not impose his views on anyone else. Nevertheless, those views are there, inside him, and every once in a while they well up: "I have to clench my fist and hold it up to my own eyes! I have to remind myself to hold my tongue. But my sons and my grandchildren look to me for my opinion before they say what is on their own minds. It was like that when I was young. My grandfather and his older brother (the man of the strap!) would come visit us, and everything stopped, while mother and father tried to get them comfortably settled in chairs, with coffee at their side. Then we would all gather around, the children, and listen to what they had to say. My grandfather was a great one for stories, and now I find myself telling the same ones to my own grandchildren. Some of them are about animals, or about the mountains, and what you must do

59

if you are to climb them and not get hurt. Some of them are about events: a trip to Albuquerque, or a time when it was so cold we all nearly froze to death.

"My great-uncle was very proud of our blood; he would argue with my grandfather right in front of us, and we would sit and watch them and forget everything else—and that does not happen often with young children! My grandfather would insist that we are American, even if we speak Spanish and come originally from Spain. My great-uncle would say that nations have empires, even when they lose the land that went to make up the empire: so long as the people are scattered all over, there is an empire. 'We are the Spanish empire,' he would say. My grandfather would then tell us children that his big brother has always been like that—a man of his own strange ideas. One time the uncle would laugh at the words of his brother, the next time he would become angry; we never knew what to expect. But they never argued for too long in front of us. They would tell each other that they would settle their differences later on. I must have been impressed; because I never have let my children see me disagree with their mother; and I notice that my sons keep quiet in front of their children, and have their fights with their wives in privacy."

Perhaps his presence is an element in his children's restraint. He wonders about that aloud, then dismisses the possibility. The issue is one of respect—how to obtain it from children, how to enable them, as they grow up and start families, to feel able to ask for it from their own children. Maybe, too, the issue is one those in a world other than his would call "cultural." Not that he, too, isn't aware of that aspect of things. He simply has his own way of getting at the subject: "We are Spanish, despite what my grandfather would say. I mean, we are citizens of this country, the United States of America; but Spain is where we all began, and Spain is here, even in this poor settlement, so unimportant that few people know us. In Albuquerque most people have never heard of our towns, even though we are only twenty or so miles east of the city. And the people of Albuquerque, so many of them, who come to these mountains to do their skiing, have no idea that some of us remember when no one wanted to slide down the sides of hills, just enjoy looking at them. Anglos cannot sit still and enjoy life. They are always on the move. Such restless people!

"I am sure that my sons will never turn into Anglo parents; they will always want to be the leaders for their children, knowing that a follower who has been well taught can become a good leader himself. When I was younger, I worked under Anglos for a while; I was a janitor, and so I came to know how they live. That was the time when money was scarce, and when I even thought of moving into Albuquerque with my family. We had our land, and we had a few chickens, but you can't live off a vegetable garden and some eggs, not with many children to raise and no work. I was lucky to get rides back and forth from here to the city, and sometimes I would sleep in the cellar—that is right, on the hard cement floor. It was stores and offices I cared for, but I would overhear them talk, those fortunate people who owned them. And believe me, they would carry their fights to work: 'I had a fight with the old lady, I told her off, I'm going to tell her off'—on and on they would go. Then they would send me out to their houses, to work on their grass or their trees, and I would hear them: such bad names they threw back and forth, and all within earshot of the children.

"Once a man told me I was lucky, because I spoke Spanish. At first I didn't quite know what he meant,

61

but he explained himself: if he and his wife spoke Spanish they could argue in Spanish, and then the children wouldn't hear every awful word. I didn't say anything—I did not want to lose my job—but I was unfit for work the rest of the day. I worried about his poor children—they were poor in a way my children weren't. (Excuse my boasting; it is bad to do, but one gets tempted and gives in.) The Anglos are always fighting at work: dog eat dog. They like to lord it over others —us, the Indians, anyone who gets in their way. And there that boss of mine was ready to take our Spanish tongue and use it to try and fool his own children! Who would be fooled? I wonder. Children don't have to understand words to know that their parents are fighting. When parents have no respect for each other, the children will pretty soon find out. I wanted to shake my fist at him and tell him that I speak English well enough to use it in a fight with my wife, but I will never do so, nor she. We might have kept a few secrets from the younger children, who hadn't started school, and so didn't know much English, but we would soon have been found out: 'Those tricky two,' the children would think to themselves, 'calling each other names in a different tongue, then telling us to be honest and conceal nothing.'

"When I came home and told my wife what the Anglo had said, she shrugged her shoulders. Later she told me I was making too much of it. (She saw I was in low spirits at supper, and had nothing to say to anyone.) She brought me my coffee and gave me a candy she'd made, and said I was playing their game by exciting myself over a few words spoken by a man who had just squabbled with his wife. 'Pity them,' my wife said. Why? I wanted to know. 'Because they have such big appetites, and still they are unhappy.' I looked confused for a second or two, and I was going to get an explanation from my wife, but by the grace of God my own head made sense of what she was saying. I realized that for the Anglo the Spanish tongue was like land: get it, get anything that there is to get, and then there will be happiness. Of course, he was an unhappy man, and I ought to have realized it then and there, and not made *myself* unhappy all day, worrying because I had heard an insult to my people's language, and not been able to reply like a man. To think that a man would want to use Spanish like a knife or a gun—something to fight with!"

Upon occasion he has talked about what it is to be a man—or a woman. He is not given to long pronouncements on the subject. For a while, in fact,—until he has met a visitor over and over again and feels ready to relax with him—he will insist that there is nothing at all to say about the subject. He will smile, then adroitly shift to another topic. Or to silence: in which case a point has been made even more emphatically. But once he did mention some differences between himself and his wife, and after that the ice seemed broken for good; he would again and again quite naturally point out that he is like this, his wife like that— and both of them true to their kind. The first moment was brief but pointed; he had dropped his pipe and tried to clean up the tobacco but without full success: "I have not my wife's patience. I will die an upset, excited man. She will die quietly. Even if, God forbid, she is in pain, she will accept the Lord's decision to test her before taking her in His hands. I will be annoyed and bitter: why is He doing this to me? Why won't He let me go quietly and without suffering? I will be trying to tame my desire to fight. How dare anyone, man or woman, fight the Lord! My wife will have no such desire to fight."

Then he looked down at the tobacco he hadn't managed to pick up or brush aside with his foot, and drew the conclusion he believed appropriate: "You see, I am really fighting with that tobacco. I want to grab it; I want to kick it and push it in a corner. And it is all my fault; the poor tobacco has no will of its own. Now, my wife would not behave this way. She would be kind toward the poor tobacco—on the floor there when it should be in my pipe. She would lean over and pick up everything without saying a word, and there would be no problem. I have watched her all these years, picking up after each one of us, and wondered whether she doesn't feel put upon. We have even had our talks about that: no, she says, anymore than I used to feel it unfair to have to go out and listen to the insults of Anglos, and clean up after them, and take care of their garbage—while she sat home and listened to the radio, the music she loves so. She would send us all off and feel like a queen, alone and with music to hear all day."

Another time that radio and its music set him going again about women and men and how they age differently. He steered himself toward the points he wanted to make with a certain easy elegance: "Music touches the soul. I cannot imagine Church without music. Soon I will die, and I will admit that I wonder what will meet me in the beyond: the fires of Hell or the peace of Heaven. When I think of Heaven I think of music —there must be good music up there. There have been times when I see my wife up there listening to music; meanwhile I am denied admission: my sins. Heaven cannot be only for women, nor Hell for men, I know, but it is a temptation to believe that is how God wills things.

"We are both old, so I guess we both think more of death. 'Do you think of death?' my sons will ask me. They mean no harm. They worry about us, and know we have little time left. I tell them no, not too much.

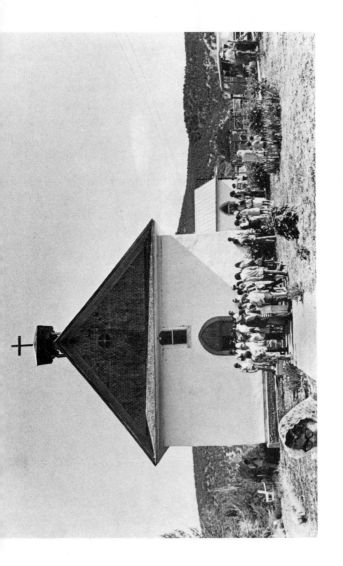

But how much is too much? I don't know. I swear, until I was seventy I never thought of death at all. Then all the celebration: my seventieth birthday. And soon we were married fifty years. I turned to my wife one day and asked her—I hesitated a good long time before I dared speak—whether she worried about dying. No, she said. But she must have known what was on my mind, because she said she had been thinking a lot about death, lately—asking herself what it would be like after the heart stops and one is no longer among the living. I asked her when she'd first had her thoughts of that kind, and she said many years ago—perhaps when she was carrying our first son, and even before that, too. I was dumbfounded. I thought she was joking. No, she wasn't, though. We had a long talk. I had never before that day realized what it is to be a man, what it is to be a woman. There are some joys to old age, but none greater than realizing that finally you are learning about the really important things. Perhaps God reveals some of His mysteries to us at the very end, before He receives us into His Kingdom—or tells us no, we do not merit it."

He is not anxious to repeat what he and his wife talked about. Certainly he is not urged to do so. No one who has met him, tall and straight for all his years, sure of himself as he talks or walks or does his chores, can imagine him being successfully urged to do anything he hasn't of his own accord decided to embark upon. He likes to drink coffee, and usually his wife keeps a pot full on the stove. But sometimes she goes to church in the morning to sit with other women and sew, and on those days he more or less fends for himself: "I went to make coffee, and saw we had run out. She will bring some home, I am sure. She thinks I drink too much of it: maybe she forgets to make me some on purpose! Women have to remember everything, it seems: Is the coffee soon to be gone, or the flour, or the sugar? They know when the end is near, when a new supply is needed.

"Men go on, fighting against the odds; it is a hard world, and each man has to carve out his small place. Women are close to the seasons; they keep their eye on the sun and they know when life is starting and when it is stopping. They bring life into the world and they care for life. They make food—and without it we die. They are always worrying that the dog has not yet come home, or a bird has fallen from a nest and needs care, or the cake didn't turn out well, or one of the children seems frail and catches too many colds. Meanwhile the men are fighting with each other to be first, or going off to a job, even if they don't like it, so that they can have money to bring home.

"I don't mean to be unfair to my own kind! I went to the doctor last month—a cold that wouldn't leave, and perhaps it was pneumonia, we began to think—and he is a man quite like my wife. Everything she had asked me, he did! I told my wife she has been my doctor for over fifty-five years! And she said yes, a woman is always watching her children and her husband: How are they breathing and how are they eating and how do they look and what do they need to look even better and feel even better? Until then I'd never realized what crosses my own wife's mind so often—and imagine, over fifty-five years together! So, we talked some more, and she told me that years ago, while I slept she would listen to me breathing, and listen to the children as they moved about in their beds, and think about each one of us: what we like to eat, and what we would be doing that might be special the next day. Or she would be thinking of someone's birthday, or whose clothes needed mending. I have always gone to sleep right away and the next thing it is morning, and my wife is shaking me and I look up and she is dressed and I can smell the coffee, good and strong. Now that I am near eighty I have at last found out what has been happening all those nights: she has slept, too, but her sleep has been different than mine, much lighter. She had too much on her mind to let herself forget everything, the way I did.

"Now that I think back, I remember that she would doze a bit in the afternoon; she would tell me when I came home that a nap of fifteen minutes after lunch and before the children came home from school was as good as a night's sleep for her. I can never sleep in the day, even now, when I have more time. After we lost a child—he would have been another son—my wife told me she wasn't sleeping well; for a month or more it lasted, though I can't say I knew much about what it was like for her at night. She did tell me once that she wasn't feeling well, and the pain had kept her up. Only now do I know that it was her sadness; she would sit and wonder what kind of boy we might have had. I had told her we already had three, and best to be grateful for them, rather than feel sorry for too long that we have lost one. But for a mother each child is precious; and she carried the boy, not me! I don't think a man can put himself in a woman's shoes; but I think a woman is always putting herself in everyone else's shoes—her children's, her husband's, her neighbor's. It is only these recent days, when we both know that soon we are to go, that we share our lives with each other in words. To be old is to be given time to remember; and if you are blessed with good health, as we are, there is also energy to share memories with one another, and with the children and grandchildren."

He stops at the mention of his grandchildren. He has memorized the total number of them (twenty-four) but he has trouble remembering which son has how many children. And he is not all that good at keeping their names in mind. Again, there is the contrast with his wife, who knows exactly how old each child is, not to mention his or her name. How does she do it, keep so much in her head? What is the matter with his own thinking? He asks those questions of himself, and sometimes of his wife, too. She laughs and tells him he is making too much out of nothing. He has worked hard all his life and given her and her children a good life. She had been home bringing up the children, thinking about them day and night; no wonder the names of the grandchildren, however many, stay with her. Nor does she let the matter drop there. For the grandchildren he is the one whose every word is heeded, and she is glad that kind of respect, even awe, still obtains in the family. "My wife says it will be a sad day when children don't hold up their fathers and grandfathers as the ones who have the last word. I tell her that it is a different age, the one we now live in. Women are the equal of men. But not in our family; not among our people here in this part of New Mexico. My sons have wives who think as my wife does, and they are not old. My sons say that their children tell them, whenever there is an argument about something, that I should be called in for advice. I say to my sons, 'You must be tired of hearing that; you must get hot under the collar.' No, they tell me they have a lot to look forward to—they will also be grandfathers one day.

"Well, I have to be honest with them; I tell them that when I was first married, my grandfather was still alive, and I remember my father bowing to his every wish and word. But I go on to say that I think there should be some changes; because a man gets old is no reason to go along with his vices. If one is of good spirit, and has lived to sort out what makes sense from what doesn't, then all very well that others pay attention. If one has had bad judgment, then long years of being a fool don't deserve to be overlooked. My sons will hear none of that, however. I only hope they are wise when they tell me that they have made their decision: I am worth their complete respect!

"Of course the grandchildren take their grandmother and me on faith. I worry that sometimes I may say something that misleads them and they will not know it. My wife asks me if I ever had such second thoughts when our own children were young. No, of course not; there was no time then for anything but work and more work. Now with age we have the luxury of many hours to think about what we have done and what we are doing, and God willing, what we will do in the time left. But I have to admit that I'm not overcome by any doubts I may have. When I go to see my sons and grandchildren I am the only person I know how to be: myself. They come to me and tell me what has happened since I last saw them, and ask me questions; and they say, please, let us have another of your stories.

"My stories: they are memories that I have accumulated, memories of a long life, and now I have use for them. The children listen so eagerly, and often I find that my son or my daughter-in-law will put aside whatever they are doing and sit with the children. It is a temptation: I carry on like a talkative priest. But later I say to myself: we are all here for God's purposes, and through me younger people can learn about what it was like in the past, and they can find out about their family. No one should want to look only to the future. If there are some people who don't care about the past, they are lost souls.

"My sons and I are more on the same footing, you could say. No longer do they keep their tongues while I use mine. I ask them what they believe, and they tell me. We usually agree, but I am glad that sometimes we don't. Then I know they will turn into their own selves: not a grandfather who is exactly like me, just as I am different from my grandfather. Mind you, not so very different; on most things I am like he was.

"I never talk about the world's problems with my wife—she has no interest in such matters; but my oldest son, especially, wants to talk about our people, and what is happening to the country, and so I join him. This is when I do more listening than is usual for an old, bossy man like me, so used to being begged for words and more words. My son has moved to Albuquerque, and even though he is living outside the city, and has his chickens and a horse and a pony, I think the city has gone to his head a bit. He works in a supermarket, and has done well for himself. He is no manager, but neither does he wash and sweep the floors, like he used to do. They have him checking out customers, and I will tell you, it is almost impossible for me to understand how he does the work: all those numbers to read and register on the machine, and all the change to make, for one customer after another. I am glad I encouraged him to stay in school; and the army helped, too: he went to school while in the service and came out sure of himself with numbers and able to take a car apart and put it together so fast you think he's a magician, watching him.

"Maybe it is the world he saw when in the army, or the people he sees all day long—maybe that is why he has such strong ideas about what is good and bad here in this state or in other parts of the country. I never did read newspapers. He does, every day. He watches television in the evenings; we love our radio. We have a television set—the gift of our second son, who works as a repair man. You can imagine how much he sees of television! I ask him whether it isn't too much, repairing the sets by day, and looking at them by night, but he says no, he is happy. Sometimes we put on the set when the children come; the grandchildren like to watch. They ask me what my favorite program is, and I tell them that I have none. They think that means I like all of them equally; it really means I know none of them.

"*Chicano,* that is the word. My sons tell me they hear it all the time, and my oldest son wants me to think of myself as a Chicano. For a while I resisted him. I said I have no interest in these words—the politicians come up with them, then throw them aside for new ones. But the boy is stubborn. He is not a boy; he is a man. And he has won me over. We are Spanish people. We are Americans. We live here up in the mountains. To tell you the truth, we belong to no town, just a few houses here on the road. But the fact is that Anglos are the rich ones; they control the county, with their money and influence. Our own people have always had a good say about what happens in this state. We have sent men to big positions: senator, as high as that. Only a handful of us are rich, though; most of us are poor. With the Anglos it's a little different. They don't have too many rich, either. The rich are always few, compared to the poor—no matter the country or the people you are talking about. But the Anglos have more people than we do who have good jobs and live well. The Anglos are favored in the schools; their language is the one that is used, and our children have to go along. My son says mostly it's Anglo managers and Chicano workers.

"I used to tell him to be glad there *is* work, but no more. One cannot go by the past. One loves the past, but one has bad memories as well as good. I don't tell my grandchildren how poor we were. We still are, but at least there is enough for food, and we live very simple lives. We ask for nothing but a little to eat and wood

71

for our fireplace and some dollars to put in the tray on Sunday. I have one suit, and it is so old I can't remember when I bought it. But I only wear it on Sundays, so it has lasted. My son would want me to have more; he thinks all our people deserve more. Who would disagree? I remember that my father would take off his hat when talking to certain Anglos, but not with our own people. That is not right, to be afraid of people.

"Mostly we have our lives up here, away from Anglos; but in the city they are everywhere, and you have to make peace with them. My younger sons, the last two, are also in Albuquerque, but they don't have much to do with Anglos, not as much as the oldest one. Maybe that is why they don't get as angry as he does. They say live and let live; the oldest one says that is fine, but you have to struggle for your rights, or else you'll be pushed aside and treated like a child. I said to him I only wish Anglos treated more of us like children; then they would be nice to us, and let us grow up and have our own lives, like children have when they get bigger. But no, too often the rich people treat the poor like dogs: 'Stay around and do my bidding and don't dare be an equal with me, because you are not, and only the scraps go to you.'

"It is all too much for me to figure out. I will say this: my sons have more to fall back on than I've ever had. They work hard, but they get more money than I ever dreamed of making. Their children are getting good educations; they look up to me, but when I hear them talking, I think to myself that it is me who should be catching *their* every word. They listen to their father, too. They tell me that I should be proud because I am a Chicano who is old and has survived all the pains of this life. I tell them that I never thought of life as painful; I lived and enjoyed myself. There was sickness and suffering, too. I remember times when

72

we never could be sure there would be food the next day. But one doesn't give up. If it will help my grandchildren to live better lives, I will call myself a Chicano and offer what strength I have left to *la causa*. I told my son as much, and he said he only wanted my approval. I embraced him for saying that."

With that he held out his arms, as if his son were there, waiting. His sons are his life, are him extended in time; in his own way he says that over and over again. If one of them thinks of himself as a Chicano, then part of him is indeed a Chicano. If another son says no, then he also has reservations about political slogans. His oldest grandson has a picture of César Chávez on his wall, and is very much a young Chicano. His oldest granddaughter is quite bright and wants to go to college. She, too, has a picture of Chávez looking down at her. She is a Chicana, and reminds her grandfather of that fact rather often: "I take her around and hug her, then I whisper to her that I am with her, and am a Chicano. She smiles."

When he is not talking about his grandchildren he is thinking of them; through them he can imagine the future. His life, he says in a sort of summary, has been "a hard one," but not so hard lately. His father and grandfather had it harder. Slowly the country has become richer, and some of the wealth—not much, but some—has filtered down. Once he smiled and became rather didactic: "I am on the bottom, and so naturally it takes time for a poor man like me to receive much of anything. I have worked all my life, and I have no regrets. I only hope that my grandchildren realize their dreams. Necessity has been my master. I have had no time to stop and ask questions. I have had no time to argue. Perhaps if I had been more like my oldest son, and if all of us my age had been like him, then we could have gained some concessions from the rich people who run businesses and run the government and decide the fate of the poor. But we did not know to fight for ourselves then. Besides, we are proud; we will not feel sorry for ourselves. Never do I want to go to someone with my hat in my hand or on my knees —never, never. I have kept quiet in the past when I wanted to shout at Anglos; but I have never lost my pride in myself in my dealings with them.

"A long time ago I asked the priest what will happen to us—so little work was to be had then, and I feared for the future of my children, and for my people all over. He said he could understand my fears. He said some priests might tell me to turn the other cheek and wait for the next world, but he wished there was some way that all of us who are living so close to hunger might find the jobs we seek, and get good wages for the hard work we're ready to do. I told him not to worry. I said we'd manage. He had started out feeling sorry for me, but I pitied him by the time we had talked a while. He seemed to regret he was a priest. He was ready, he told me, to take off his collar and become a fighter on our behalf. I said no, we would fight for ourselves, and not be beaten. I think I was only pretending when I said that; I had no reason to be hopeful then.

"But we never quite lost all hope, even during the worst of times. My grandfather used to say to me when I was but a boy that our people have been living on this land here in New Mexico for a long, long, time— many generations, back and back and back in time. Only the Indians were here before us. The Anglos came much later. So, we will not leave, and we will somehow keep ourselves alive. Necessity demands it. When the belly sends messages that it hurts, the man works harder to get food. He plants, he harvests. He keeps after his chickens. He gets a job, even if the pay is very little. There are times when I want to tell my sons how lucky they are that necessity has let up on their generation. They have time to enjoy life, and to ask all the questions they now come up with: Why are things the way they are, why don't we have more to say in what happens to our people?"

He stops and thinks; then he wonders out loud what the answers to such questions are. He shakes his head. He puts his right hand through his hair. Suddenly he feels to blame—though for what he is not sure. His hair: perhaps it is not yet white at his age because he did not worry enough in the past about some of the issues that preoccupy his oldest son. Perhaps he ignored what was right in front of him—so much injustice, so much exploitation—in order to go his own way from day to day.

But no, he will not criticize himself unfairly. He stands up straight and holds both of his hands out as he talks: "A man does not become eighty in order to spend his last precious hours having regrets and calling himself bad names. We all stand on the shoulders of others. My grandfather used to hold me on his shoulders and tell me to put my arms around his head as if it were a steering wheel. Then he would carry me, and I would point the direction. When we got to our destination, he would put me down and say he was ready to take me back when I wished. Then he would help me climb a tree or carve some wood. I remember looking at that knife of his and wishing that someday I might have one like it. And the day came: he died and my father was given the knife and he came to me and said I was the oldest boy, and so I could have it—but for a while I had to share it with him. Now it is my first grandson's. Now I carry him on my shoulders. Each of us is given so far we can go—so much time, so much energy. We do our best, then stop and say good-bye. When I am on my

75

deathbed, I will think of my wife and my children and my grandchildren, and I will say good-bye to them all, and I will picture the young ones, my sons and my grandsons and granddaughters, walking further up the road, and then one day the sons will have to say good-bye to *their* children, and so it goes."

He stops and returns to his seat. Some coffee he had been holding has now grown cold. He empties it and gets himself some more. It is chilly outside, an early February morning. But he loves to face down weather, however severe. So long as he is able, he will do chores, walk, greet neighbors, wave at children, give horses sugar, scold chickens for being lazy and threaten them with an hour or two in the oven. If one is to enjoy the radio's music, take a good rest in the afternoon, one must venture forth in the morning. That is how he believes he should spend his remaining days, and that is also how a life should be spent: a good deal of work, followed by a well-earned rest.

He tells his children what his philosophy is and they nod enthusiastically: "I say to them that they must prepare for the future; they must know how to be on time for appointments, and ready to give all the energy they have to the work they do. My grandson says he will go to the university and work hard there. I tell him that will be wonderful. Then he tells me that no matter what he learns there, he will still look up to me. I say that is also wonderful—and I pick him up and show him I still have some strength left in my arms. Then I put him down and tell him I had a teacher all my life, even though I had so little schooling: necessity is a demanding teacher. Yes, the boy agrees. Then I boast; it is bad to do, but I can't control myself. *Enseña más la necesidad, que un año de universidad.* How would an Anglo say it? Necessity teaches more than one year of university study? Yes, that is what I say. My wife tells me I should be ashamed of myself, bragging like that, but I want the children to know that their grandfather has a useful life. And they are not bothered by what I say. They clap their hands and say hurrah! And I clap back at them."

4

# THE AGE OF
# A REPUTATION

Even people who work the land buy food at stores if they have any money at all. In the countryside of the South, in Appalachia, and in the semidesert country of New Mexico the store that rural people frequent is at once a source of needed supplies and a location where people meet and exchange news and gossip—a center of community life, really, and often the place one gets mail, emergency phone calls, messages of various kinds from relatives in the far-off city. A visitor who comes to a particular community or settlement in a large but for the most part thinly populated state like New Mexico in hopes of understanding how certain families live does well to make the acquaintance of the man and woman (usually it is both) who run the market or grocery store (the names seem interchangeable). One such store is called just that: "The Store." Most of the customers who go to that particular store are Spanish-speaking, as are the owners; but Indians and Anglos also come by. The owner is Señor Gallegos; for a long time he was called Mike, but as he grew older

77

and older, he became Señor Gallegos to everybody, and his oldest son, who works with him, became Mike. Señora Gallegos, who for years has stood behind the counter alongside her husband, has never been anything but Señora Gallegos to her customers.

For a time, when she was bearing and rearing children, Señora Gallegos had a limited number of hours to spend in the store. The family has always lived in a house that connects to the store, and the children, even as infants, often played there. But their mother was strict and attentive: there were just so many liberties they were allowed, and she made sure *she* had a liberty —the right to gather herself and the children up and leave at moments when the store threatened to turn into a noisy nursery. As the children—four girls, three boys—grew up, their mother spent longer and longer uninterrupted stretches of time waiting on customers, and now she has more say than her husband about what happens in the store. "I am a year his senior," she explains, "but God has seen fit to keep me looking younger than him." Then she speaks of a certain irony in her life and his: "We are both over eighty, but I will not say by how much. I have never wanted to talk about age. It is a subject that brings up memories. Even after all these years I can still remember my mother asking me why I wanted to marry a man who was younger than I. And my husband, what he didn't hear from his mother—and his father, too! We both were made to think we were sinful. Imagine! When people have their ideas, they don't like anyone to disagree. The man should be older than the woman, that is what my parents and my husband's parents believed. They even went to the priest. What to do about this scandal?

"The old priest understood how they felt, but he told them that they were being foolish. I think he used that very word—my mother told me so, much later. He said it is foolish to let a year's time become a judgment on two people who love each other. With that, we were able to get married, and there was no trouble afterward. I can still remember, though, how people felt before we were married: I was a stained woman who was capturing a *boy;* and my husband, he was a nice child, innocent as could be, who was allowing himself to be tricked. It was an awful time, and for a while I wanted to say no, and never get married. I talked to the priest about becoming a nun, but he was so very helpful and wise: one doesn't turn to God because one has had trouble with one's friends and neighbors—that is what he told me, and I shall never forget his eyes, full of affection and understanding. Then I stiffened my back and decided to go ahead, and so did my husband; and here we are, sixty years later!

"For some strange reason I have always felt younger and been taken as younger than my husband. For a while I began to believe that it was God's way of punishing all the people who told stories about us and winked and showed those smiles that were meant to say: we know about those two! The priest told me to stop having such an idea about God; He has other things to do than help me get revenge on some idle, gossipy people who have no charity or kindness in their hearts. So, it is simply fate: my husband's to grow weak in his old age, and begin to lose his memory; and as for me, I still have a lot of my black hair, my teeth haven't fallen out, and I am sure that my head is still in good condition. After all, I can keep track of all the price changes these days, and that requires plenty of fast thinking. Last week my husband had one of his spells; he can be all right for a while, but then he goes back in time, and suddenly a customer is being told that she can have a loaf of bread for a dime, and the milk is that, too—or maybe fifteen cents. I have to

79

humor him; I have to be gentle. I will tell him to stop trying to be funny, or stop having a daydream, and usually he will smile, and be grateful to me for helping him without causing any shame. And the customer will sigh and say, 'One day in the future it will be nice to have such prices'—something like that.

"My older sister—she is nearing ninety—tells me that I have been rewarded for being a good wife and mother: God has given me health and kept me young. I do not like her to talk like that. My husband has been a fine person all these years. I cannot imagine a life without him. If he has not been allowed to stay in the best of health lately, it is no reflection on his goodness. The wicked can often prosper; the finest of people can suffer terribly. I remind my sister of our Lord's life— so short; then she tells me to stop, and that way she has admitted her error.

"My sister is an inspiration to me; I don't mean to speak ill of her. She lost her husband many years ago; he had pneumonia and died. He was forty-five, I think. There were no doctors near here; there still aren't any. We couldn't get one to come and see him. The priest told me there was little a doctor could do; there was a crisis, and either one lived or died. Today they have good medicines; he would have lived—though we still cannot get a doctor to come visit, if someone suddenly becomes seriously ill. We would have to drive the person to Española. Since her husband's death, all these years ago, my sister has brought up a family, and helped us in the store. It was her idea to start cutting the hair of children; mostly in the town it is done at home by parents, but some fathers say no, and some mothers are not very good with the scissors—the children cry or fuss, and the mothers get nervous. My sister had been helping several of our cousins to cut their children's hair; she had always been so fast and in control of herself when she clipped—and in control of the boys and girls, too. When her husband died, they wanted to pay her. She said no. They pleaded. She said no.

"One day a mother came to her, not a relative, and asked for her help. The mother was afraid she'd hurt her children. As for her husband, he had epilepsy, and she was afraid he'd get a fit while holding the scissors over the heads of their children—and then, oh then! My sister reassured her; her trouble seemed to be her imagination—her 'fear,' my sister called it. My sister told her to bring the children to the store, and we brought a chair in and put it over in the corner there, an empty space, and put a table beside it, with a bowl— and soon the children had their haircuts. In the time it takes to blink the whole village knew, and the same thought came to everyone: my sister is wonderful with children who need to have their hair cut, and it is a polite way to be of help to her—the children to raise, and a husband taken away so early in life. And so she became a barber! The young priest here laughs; he says that all over America women are unhappy with their lives, and want more respect; and he says they should take their example from my sister who has performed the work of men for long years, and for doing so never paraded herself as someone special.

"For a time, before she became too old—her hands started shaking—she cut the hair of grown men, too. They would bring their children, and then they would begin teasing her, and saying, 'If you can work on them, why not on us?' So, she said yes, she would work on them, if they promised not to be vain and complain about the result. That is how my sister became a barber —when she wasn't being a mother and one of the people who runs this store. I believe on my deathbed I will think of her talking to our cousin one day long ago. He is probably the worst customer she has ever had; he cares about his appearance much too much. She has always tried to obey his instructions, but he has always wanted himself to be the most handsome man ever put here on New Mexico's land, and because he must realize that there are hundreds of miles between his wishes for himself and the way he looks to our eyes, he has to have someone to accuse: it is you or you or you who ruin my looks. Either his wife is scolded for keeping him fat, or someone like my poor sister is scolded.

"Well, the day I remember was rainy; we don't have much rain here. He had his haircut and he stood there looking at the weather outside. He had no hat, and he would look awful by the time he got home. I offered him my husband's hat, but he realized then what a peacock he was being. No, he would just go; but could he at least look at himself in a mirror, so that he would have the satisfaction of knowing what a good job my sister, his beloved cousin, had done? I winked at my sister and went to get a mirror. He looked. His face fell. Oh, how sad; too much had been removed. A pity! My sister stared right at him and replied, 'Dearest cousin, do not worry. A barber's mistakes grow out. A doctor's, the patient carries to the grave; and a priest's can lead one to Hell.' He sat up and took her around and said she was a wise woman. I will say so! And she still is, even at ninety.

"The other day I asked her how she can be in such good spirits; she has bad arthritis, and her digestion is not of the best. 'My sister,' she said, 'my life is not mine; it belongs to God. I am afraid to die. I do not want to die. I cannot persuade myself to like being old. I am no magician who can make a trance for herself, and end up welcoming what is a fearful moment: the last breath. But I have been given ten years short of a century already, and I don't seem to be leaving yet,

82

for all my aches and pains. I am rich with years, a millionaire! I have been part of my own generation, then I watched my children's generation grow up, then my grandchildren's, and now my great-grandchildren's. Two of my great-grandchildren are becoming full-grown women now; they come visit me, and will remember me. Now, I ask you, how much more can a woman expect? My great-granddaughter told her teacher I was a barber fifty years ago, and the teacher wanted to send my name to Santa Fe, and they would honor me as a pioneer among women. Well, imagine that! I said no. I have been honored already—all this life I've been given is an honor God has chosen to offer. It is a big achievement, if I say so myself, to have accumulated all these years. And as I look back and think, I decide that I wouldn't have done things any different, not for the most part, anyway.'

"I am taking liberties with what she said, but I can remember her words, because my head tries hard to hold on to almost every one of them. I told my husband her message, and he nodded. I thought: It will not stay with him; he only keeps the old memories. But yesterday he said she is a wise woman, my sister— for two days he had been thinking of her speech to me. 'Do you think we should be proud, too, even if we have a few more years until we're her age?' he asked me. I didn't answer him. He didn't need an answer. I hugged him—oh, I was ashamed for a second, because my son walked in, and so did a customer. 'So, that's how you two mind the store for me,' our son said. And the customer, she was a young woman carrying her first child, and she said she had something to dream about now: if only she and her husband could live so long and still feel love for each other. I told her not to worry. God can be generous, even if there are disappointments and sadness in this life, too."

She may be stronger than her husband, but she still defers to him. She will make a remark about God and His loving-kindness, then look to Señor Gallegos for confirmation. Sometimes she will even ask "Yes?" of him. Usually he quickly gives what is requested of him, but once in a while he demurs. He does so by not saying anything for what strikes a visitor as rather a long time. Meanwhile his wife has quite clearly understood what he is up to. She moves toward him and begins to explain herself further. Her voice becomes not so much plaintive as appeasing, and also, reassuring: perhaps I have been a bit brusque, a bit inconsiderate in the way I throw off these remarks—and you, so busy working, for all the frailty of your years!

He does work. He opens up the store every morning at seven. He has already been up two, maybe three hours. He needs little sleep these days. His thoughts are pulled back at four or five in the morning to his childhood and youth; and, to a degree, he doesn't mind; he even enjoys recalling old experiences, visualizing faces long since gone. But eventually he is grateful for the requirement of work. If left to his mind's inclination he might never return to the year 1973. So, up he is, and soon at the stove making oatmeal—for sixty years his breakfast, regardless of the weather, the season—and drinking his black coffee. He has his ailments, but his stomach is in excellent shape. He takes coffee. He loves chili, the hotter the better—sometimes even for breakfast. When he himself feels his mind getting especially foggy or drawn to the past, he leaves the store and takes some chili, followed by bread without butter. The chili livens up his thinking, he is sure. And he does indeed seem more agile, more alert on his return. Who is his visitor, aware of what is peddled to millions of aging Americans in the name of aids for "fitness" or a

84

youthful appearance, to come up with a note or two in his diary about Señor Gallegos's "superstitions"?

By dawn "the Señor," as his wife sometimes calls him in front of a visitor, has opened the store, put the daily five dollars of change in the various compartments of the cash register, crossed off the previous day on the calendar, and prepared himself for the first customer. That is the expression he uses: "prepare myself." One wonders why. Without being asked, he satisfies his guest's curiosity: "There are so many things to sell, and the prices do not stay the same. I like to keep the store clean. I like the first customer to come in and feel he is entering a home—spotless. I make a big pot of coffee; for years I have offered morning coffee. I like it myself. I like others to have it. For a while they wanted to pay, but I wouldn't hear of it. They will buy doughnuts, though. I have the radio going. I could put on television, but that is for later. The people who come by early do not want to look; they would rather listen. We don't talk much. In the early morning people are quiet. It is later in the day that children come in with their mothers or alone, and then it livens up. At seven the sun is up, but we are all still shaking off sleep—even me, and I've been up a couple of hours by then.

"The people near here like to come by every day. Some mothers send their husbands to the store each morning before breakfast. No wonder I have to be ready for them; they expect me to know by heart what they will be asking for. And why not? After all these years I'd be of no use if I couldn't predict what my customers want and need. Still, with age one has to think a little harder. So, about six-thirty I am picturing the men, and looking at the shelves to see that I have what they'll come for. Usually they don't even have to talk much when they enter. I look at them and go for the milk or some cereal or some cans—and of course,

85

I have the doughnuts near the coffee. They put the money for the doughnuts in the glass jar; that is separate. The rest I ring up.

"We charge more than the big markets in the city. We must. We don't get to buy at the low prices a chain of stores can make the wholesale people set. Maybe one day there will be no stores like ours left. I apologize all the time to my customers. I tell them that if they would only drive twenty miles, they could do better. I know that some storekeepers like me have a fine time bleeding their customers—the people who can't travel or are in a hurry for something. But it is not in me to run that kind of business. I am too old to do a dance because I squeezed an extra nickel here, and a quarter there, out of some neighbors of mine. I would have nightmares, thinking of what they wished me: a long stretch in Hell. And I would belong there!

"The older I become, the more I think of others. Have I been a good husband and a good father? Will my friends think well of me when the casket with me in it moves down the street toward the cemetery? What will my cousins and my nephews and nieces and my neighbors and customers think when they stand there and see me put to rest: 'He is a scoundrel who took away from the poor and cheated people by touching the scale with his hand and raised prices far beyond what was fair?' or 'He did the best he could, and tried to be honest, and had a smile on his face most of the time?' I cannot say for sure; maybe I have been more thoughtless and rude than I will ever know. When God gives you the extra time he has given me, it may be because he expects you to examine yourself very closely, and think about what you have done wrong. I know that when I was younger I worried about money: I wanted there to be some for our old age. Back then I thought: If we live to be sixty-five, or seventy, we will be lucky, and we will no doubt be weak and so our son will have to run the store all by himself. But we lived longer, and here I am, still opening the store, so that my son can have a decent sleep, and see his children off to school.

"I didn't grow rich; nor will my son. He would like to make more money, I know. He resembles me; he is torn between the desire to make money for his wife and children, and a great loyalty to our customers. How can you take more than is due you—especially when you know you are lucky to have the store and live comfortably as you do, and many of your customers aren't all in the same shoes? I have no answers; I wish everyone in the world had enough to eat, good clothes, and a roof that doesn't leak over their heads. I tell our priest all the time that it is no joy, taking money from people who don't have much, and who work so hard for the little they do have. He slaps me on the back and tells me that it is not me or Señora Gallegos or our son who are the enemies of the poor. He tells me about other stores he knows of, from his past work: the owners are politicians, and they push the people around and take every cent they can get. I feel good, hearing him speak well of me, but I still worry: God must know that I have had my moments of greed.

"There have been people I have not liked, and they have pushed me hard: Why do you charge such high prices? Why do you try to bleed us? I have tried to answer: it is trying and lonely running a store like this one, and if I give everything away, I will have to beg myself, rather than run the store. But I can hold firm; no one will knock me down, not when I think I am in the right. Sometimes I feel ready to fight; and sometimes I have said to myself, 'Take all you can get, because they are mean ones, and they will only respect a man who is as mean as they are.' And you know, that is true:

there are people on this earth who have contempt for a man who tries to be generous; he is seen as a fool, or up to some clever trick. That is God's way—to put many different kinds of people here, and let us all prove ourselves before him."

He stops and adjusts his suspenders. It is as if he is worried: how does *he* look before God? How has *he* managed to "prove" himself, all these years? He feels his face: old as he is, he still has to shave, and every other day is not enough. He takes out his handkerchief, unfolds it, then folds it up again—a habit of his that his wife for a long time tried to break, then came to appreciate: his way of arranging and rearranging, and certainly of no harm to anyone. He moves toward the shelves, spots a can of peaches out of place, puts it back with the others, does the same with some cans of soup, and soon is standing near the cash register, his fingers playing on the keys. His daughter plays the piano; she bought a small one for her children, and has learned to play it herself. His piano is that cash register; it is a wonder, he observes, that the keys are still there; all the use over all those years.

Sometimes he sees people looking at the tray; he knows they wish they had the money inside—not that they would ever make a try to take anything. They are simply good friends who are human enough to know envy or lust. Besides, they are likely to be needy. Their eyes wander toward the tray only briefly, and he has learned never to let them catch him catching them. He can see them beginning to take note of the money, and then at all costs he finds some excuse to look away from them. He has taught his son to do likewise. He has also taught his son to be tough with wholesalers, easy with those who require something and don't have ready cash. There are no "charge accounts," but he does write down sums on slips of paper—and "the next time" the customer will pay, or "the time after that." He has never refused a customer anything. He would first close up the store. He may not be the most generous man in the world, but to turn away someone in need of food is simply wrong by his standards. As for his "people," those who come to his store and salute him warmly or with casual friendliness, he has no idea what they think of him, what they *really* think of him, what they say behind his back, never mind to his face, when he knows they will be polite.

He would like to think, though, that he will be missed when he goes, and that under difficult circumstances, as a storekeeper who attends to people who are not very prosperous, he has done his work reasonably well: "I have wanted to be of some help to others, even if it is true that I make a living out of doing so. A man has to make a living. In this country people are not encouraged to work for one another— to share and live as brothers and sisters, the way our Lord Jesus Christ would no doubt wish. My grandfather told me, 'Everyone for himself in America, but don't be *too* American!' I will not speak like that to my own grandchildren. I am confused myself how much to share with others, how much to keep for myself. Why confuse little boys and girls? There will be plenty of time for them to look around and figure out the answer to the important question: How do I make a good living in this country, and still keep some respect for myself and feel I am a Christian? I wish I could give them the answer in words; but I think you get the answer through living—it takes a lifetime to find out, and maybe after all those years you still don't really know how to conduct yourself in every situation.

"Well, I hope I have achieved a good reputation. A reputation takes time to establish. A reputation has an age, just as a person does. I hope my wife and I have earned some trust from our neighbors. My father would say to me, and I say to my son, *'Cobra buena fama y acuéstate a dormir, cóbrala mala y arranca a huir.'* That is our way of saying: If you have built a good reputation up for yourself, you can feel comfortable, but if you haven't, and people think ill of you, you had better leave. This I can say: we have stayed, Señora Gallegos and I."

5

# THE OLD CHURCH, THE SPANISH CHURCH, THE AMERICAN CHURCH

In every town up in the hills of northern New Mexico or hidden among the mountains east of Albuquerque, the Catholic church is the tallest, most noticeable building to be seen. Some of the churches are nondescript, some are surprisingly flimsy: wood covered with shingles, or else brick put together without any real thought of beauty, or even, it seems, permanence; signs announcing the times of mass hung loose or crooked; no effort at landscaping, hence muddy, rutted roads in winter, or dry, dusty ones in summer—and a lonely, stark quality which a few trees might have diminished. Other churches are quite different; they are made of adobe or a mixture of adobe and cement, and are sturdy, fitting well into the town's setting, which is often evocative of the center of Spanish cities: the narrow streets, the plaza, the protective walls, and at the center of it all, His building, with the invariable announcement in Spanish (and sometimes but not always in English) that He will be worshipped at such-and-such times, and with the bell that doesn't hesitate to call on His behalf, and is immediately heeded. These are the churches that are likely to have nicely cared for grass—not to be taken for granted in semiarid country. Frequently there is also a small garden—a few cactus plants, some rocks arranged in a pleasing way. And there are usually trees, often quite massive, the best of the region's cottonwoods, for instance—and one is likely to look at them, admire them, wonder whether they haven't been put there especially to guard the church.

In the mountain communities everyone goes to church on Sundays, but there is no traffic jam as a result. The roads, so empty at times that they seem a pure indulgence on the state's part, suddenly are full of men, women, and children walking in the middle: what better use for asphalt than to help keep special clothes looking good before and after mass? As for anyone who happens to be driving toward the church, let him dare use his horn or try to nudge people with his noisy, racing motor or his tires coming rudely close. For that matter, a distant plane can receive a look meant not to kill, but merely to register the pain, confusion, and sorrow one world feels for another: how can it be that on a Sunday like this, which God has chosen to grace with His sun and with a cloudless sky, they are up there in that machine, rather than somewhere on this earth, praying?

Of course, such a question often goes unasked, merely kept in the back of the mind—a thought of sorts about the twentieth century, with its increasingly hard-to-fathom but inescapable contrasts. Time was when Santa Fe and Albuquerque were there, all right, but of no particular consequence or immediacy in the lives of various villagers for whom thirty or fifty miles might well have been three or five hundred miles. Time was when everything outside a given town's land was a limitless and not especially inviting beyond. Now there are planes, and increasingly noisy and aggressive automobile drivers, who, it seems, will no longer rest content with the usual tourist spots, but have to poke and pry their way into every corner of every county—even up dirt roads, so they can get what they call a "view." What to do but pray for them on Sundays? One may not really feel so inclined, but that is the point of prayer, to ask the hard things of God, not simply to beg in a self-centered manner for any little possession the mind may have come up with as desirable. "As the good priest says"; "as the father told us"; "as we heard in church"—the phrases vary, but they all are meant to indicate how carefully a person has listened to, and made his own, ideas handed down by another: him who helps us, leads us, urges us on to God.

"I am an instrument of the Lord's," one priest says, but not boastfully. Not coyly either; he is being matter-of-fact. "I try to do what I hope is likely to serve God's will best," he elaborates. Not that he *knows;* one can only try, and one can only hope, and one can only make a judgment about a likelihood. Then he quite consciously skirts egotism: "I have no right to set myself apart from other priests. We all fail every day, certainly those who presume to speak on behalf of our Lord. But a long time ago I think I did learn one lesson: be firm with people, stand fast for what is right, but take care not to confuse yourself with God. It is a sin even to suggest that a priest does that, but we are all tempted, and no one more than a priest, I am afraid. Some priests more than others, though; it is well to be blunt. Maybe I am the worst of us all—sitting here and making my comments about 'them' and about myself. Beware of the preacher, especially one as old and ingrained in his habits as I am."

A nervous smile is followed by a serious, reflective look, then a broader, more relaxed smile. Hands hold on to a chair; one of them quickly moves toward the right thigh, to brush aside some dust on the pants, caught by a sunbeam. Soon the hands are folded around the belly, which possesses a certain prominence: a perfect resting place for the forearms as well as the fingers. A few remarks about one parishioner, then another, and, as always, blessings on both of them: "May God offer them His grace; they are among the oldest who come here on Sundays, and I always seek them out after I talk to the people: make my announcements, deliver my sermon, offer my congratulations and give my warnings—a dangerous moment for a priest, I am convinced. For a long time I never gave a second thought to what my words meant to people; I was too busy preparing the speech and in my mind giving it. By the time I *did* give it, I had already decided whether it was one of the better ones, or one of the less useful ones. But I have been given enough time to look back and take stock—a mixed blessing, I assure you. Some of my former sermons, like ghosts, have come to haunt me. I preached charity with a complete lack of it; and mind you, I am no stranger here, but a man who ought to understand his own people."

With that, silence; a hard silence to interrupt with a clever bit of nonsense or a face-saving compliment which would only make matters worse by suggesting that self-criticism requires reassurance or is a subtle, self-assertive maneuver aimed at obtaining praise. The head bows, but not for any embarrassing length of time. A glance at the crucifix on the opposite wall, then a direct stare at the visitor, followed by an inquiry:

shall some tea be brought in? Yes; so he is up and out of the room for a second. Soon an elderly lady brings in a tray. On it, besides the tea, are an assortment of cookies and some cake, too. He looks at them, casts a quick look at his belly, then smiles at himself indulgently and reaches for the tray—to serve, but also to eat heartily. Just as the lady is leaving he refers to her, and she leaves hearing—not for the first time, one is sure—his comment: "I am a spoiled child, an old, old, one, but that is all the worse. And she is the one who does it!"

When the door is firmly closed he continues, perhaps hoping she can hear, anyway: "The two of us should stay away from such sweet things. I do not weigh myself because it is rather prideful to do so; but I know deep within my heart that I am playing a wicked game: my pride urges me to avoid facing the scale, and I call upon 'the sin of pride' as an excuse. It may be a devious move on my part, but I doubt the good Lord fails to see through my purposes. And all the time my lady friend, so anxious to care for me, urges me on to greater excesses: not only cookies, but her tasty cake! She knows only too well how weak I am; and I can't blame her, tempted though I am to do so. She offers, but I need not accept. Anyway, I have joined her in a conspiracy: I make sure she finishes what I don't. As you can see, neither of us is lean and hungry. I fear there will be a lot of fat to burn in Hell all too soon—for we are both about to go there in the near future, I would think."

Another pause, this time followed by a sigh not in the least stifled; then he shifts to a more philosophical vein: "There's no point worrying about the future. That is one of the virtues of our Spanish heritage: we are not lazy; we work hard; but we trust in God, not our own dreams of glory. Anglos believe in themselves. I should not say it, but I will: even Anglos who are Catholic do not

94

think as we do. I would go further and add Anglo *priests* to the list. Irish priests come here and the people submit to them—yes, they do—but they do not really follow them spiritually. It is difficult for me to talk like this; I find it hard to explain what I mean in English—or in Spanish either. Some might say I am getting old—over seventy, and so given to sentiment, exaggeration, melodrama. I will stand up for my beliefs, though. For almost a half century I have been a priest here in New Mexico, always with my own Spanish-speaking people, always in the small towns, where the culture and traditions and customs are most pure and least influenced by the Anglo Americans. (They call us all those names; well, I have always liked to call *them* Anglo Americans, and I think of myself as a Spanish American.) Now in all these years I have learned more than I have taught. I have come to know the people; after all, I hear their confessions and they come to me every day for advice. But I must never forget how much they have helped me to understand my own life—what my parents brought me up to believe, why I think the way I do about so many issues.

"I suppose I would be considered by some Anglo priests strict, by others far too lenient. I have no use for many of the changes now taking place in the American Church. I am grateful for being up here, far removed from those changes. I am grateful for being old; I will soon go—well before the Catholic Church I love so much becomes before our very eyes conquered by the American evangelists: practical-minded businessmen; university agnostics; experts in technology; and, I have to say it, the psychiatrists and Unitarians and—what do they call it?—'ethical culture' people, with their talk of 'community.' You see, the hippies have come near here, with their communes. I have talked with them. They give me things to read, while all the time

95

denouncing books. So I keep up with the world! The children of hippies, I fear, are lost: they know too much, have seen too much. They have no knowledge how to control themselves, only give way to their own demands. How sad, to see seven- or eight-year-old children so sure of themselves, so cynical, so demanding and bossy with strangers. But I do not want to sound shrill and narrow about hippies. The truth is, I feel sorry for them. I pray every day for them. I know they don't want my pity and my prayers. I know the danger of smugness. Still, I must pray.

"I read magazines; I have tried to keep my mind open—without success, no doubt many would say. I love the Latin mass. So do our people here. They do not want English or Spanish; they want their Latin mass— it truly is *theirs*. And they go to church to pray to God, not to man, not to the society. I did not become a priest in order to celebrate man; nor do my parishioners come here to stare in the mirror and exult at their 'capacities.'

"I respect each generation's right to see things in a new way. But the Catholic Church is devoted to one Man, who turned out to be God Himself. If we fail to center our attention on Him and His teachings; or if we go against His teachings for the sake of keeping up with 'modern times,' then it is best we close all our churches and say there is no longer a Catholic Church, just a collection of buildings to which egoists and materialists take themselves on Sundays out of some nostalgia, or because they get bored, or because they have a 'religious need,' and are trying to give it 'expression.'

"Oh, I have to tell you that I have no patience with all that. A few years ago, before I became hopelessly old-fashioned—and even bitter, I would have to admit —I would go to retreats, or to conferences; I would listen to lectures about the 'new' Church, and I would

96

try hard to go along. But I know a Protestant when I see one—even up here they have made their inroads! And I know a truly agnostic or atheistic person. I don't want to win such a person over. I respect them—that may well be one way I differ (in the more 'free-thinking' direction) from some other priests. I simply want to stand up for my own beliefs, and I do not want to fool myself or fool the families who come here by giving the name Catholic to a porridge of secular notions, any of which may be valuable and important, but none of which are meant to be worshipped in Christ's name, in the name of our Lord and Savior."

He stops, and seems to be going into a moment of intense self-absorption. He looks up at a picture of the Bleeding Heart of Jesus; it was given to him by one of the better-off families. The man and his wife had gone to Mexico and South America, and while there had remembered him. They made sure he hung the picture where he would be able to look and look—and be some-how affected. He had once before told the story: how they were so proud to have the gift for him, how they chose a place for it, having been given carte blanche with his walls, how the señora personally hung the picture, having had it framed in Santa Fe. Now, as he stared, the Bleeding Heart seemed a refuge for him: let others make their "adjustments" to the twentieth century; let others be embarrassed by the ancient imagery and ritual of Catholicism; let others feel more comfortable with toned-down iconography or updated theology or scripture interpreted defensively in the face of convictions asserted by theoretical physicists, paleontologists, observers of African chimpanzees, Marxist historians, ever so knowing and self-conscious psychoanalysts, the last with their nervy interest in a dozen other "fields," including his own. He would not wince at that representation of the Bleeding Heart, not run in shame from it, nor "reinterpret" it, nor fit it into someone's "archetypal pattern." He would simply look and meditate and gain strength. "The Lord's agony has meant peace and wisdom for millions over the years," he had said several months earlier, after a similar moment spent with that picture; now a moment was becoming a minute, which can be a long time indeed when two people are alone and talking.

Then abruptly, words begin to come—and forcefully: "I will surprise you. I acknowledge superstition within the Church. There was a time when I wanted to study philosophy and theology—not be a parish priest. And I did, by myself. There was a time, even decades ago, before the recent changes in the Church, when I had little use for those flaming fires, those blood-drenched Hearts. My father was well-to-do—a prosperous landowner, and a self-educated man. He never left the Church, but he did business with the Anglos—too much business. He made too much money, and their Protestant ideas went to his head. My mother prayed for him. Only in his last year did he really become part of the Church again. He taught me to distrust the excesses: the festivals and cards and pictures and what he called 'the smell of ignorance and fear' that hovered over the church and the parish house all week.

"My mother said, 'Why not?' She said, 'Is it better to crave the newest automobile, or a machine that washes clothes?' She loved her scrubboard. She had no use for servants. She loved her rosary beads. She hated gasoline fumes and would stop by the side of the road and pick up trash left there. That was a long time before we ever heard of the word 'ecology.' She worried that the people of this town would soon be hanging pictures of cars on their walls, rather than the Bleeding Heart of Jesus. She worried that the president would come before Christ, the skyline of Albuquerque before the

Church's mission. She was educated by nuns, and no doubt they were hard on her. But she knew how hard used-car salesmen can be on their customers, and politicians can be on the voters, and the commercials on radio can be on a poor worker, trying to keep his self-respect and trying to live a decent, honorable life. Thank God she never lived to see television. I watch it and ask, Who is superstitious, who is ignorant, who is backward: an old lady coming to me holding on to her rosary or doing a Novena or handing cards with Christ's face or His heart to her children and grandchildren, or those people who write the commercials and speak them and act in them, or worse, listen to them, then jump to pay attention?

"But I am ready to go back on my own ideas; to a degree I am. I know that I am old, and I have never done much, only take care of the souls God has entrusted to me. This world is full of injustice, and I haven't done much to change things. I preach. I ask the members of my flock to be kinder to one another. I ask them to look with care at *me:* am I mistaken in my ideas? They become uncomfortable when I talk like that. After the sermon they say, 'Father, you cannot mean what you say! Father, you must know you cannot be wrong!' I reply, 'So, you think I am dishonest when I ask you to question me!' That makes them stop and think! There is so far I have gone, though. I haven't marched to the cities with words of protest. I haven't tried to become a Chicano, a fighter in the world of politics and social activism. Christ fought the money-lenders. I know that. Christ was turned upon by the 'powers and principalities.'

"I do not deny the Church's responsibility: to be on the side of the poor, the hungry, the downtrodden. Here, of course, most people are barely able to get by, day after day. There are few rich people, and not many like my parents were—the middle class, they could be said to come from. No matter: our people are stubborn about their lives; what they have inherited they will keep, and what others want for them, they will look at with great suspicion. Am I the one to shout at them, call them fools, backward fools? Am I the one to demand that they stop being so grateful for so little, and instead, rise up, start marching, tear aside the curtains of self-doubt and hopelessness, begin forcing themselves and their reasonable and just demands upon today's pharisees and moneylenders, upon today's Pontius Pilates and the emperors who employ them?

"Any curate worth his salt tries to arouse his people; but he is also bound to feel their presence and respond to their view of life—as opposed to his own wishes for them. I will tell you: in the 1930s, when it was much more desperate a time than now, I stormed about, I was ready to lead an army down from this hill. Don't ask me where we would have gone. It never came to that. And it wasn't rich people or a sheriff who turned anyone back. There was no one to turn back. Maybe some today would say I should have raised my voice even louder, or if that failed to arouse people, march by myself. Maybe some would say I should have left here —told them all how ignorant and unimaginative they are, how little vision and little ambition they possess. I might have found willing supporters in Santa Fe, among the comfortable artists and writers, and those who hang onto them, look up to them as *their* priests. In more recent times I might have gone to Albuquerque, a noisier, less settled city, not so self-assured and full of itself, not so interesting to Easterners—and a place where a justifiably angry priest, anxious to link arms with his people's forward-looking organizers and spokesmen, might be quite welcome. I am glad, very glad, there are priests who have done so—become leaders of the very broadest kind. If I get sullen and meanspirited, if I try to protect myself, justify myself, by saying uncharitable, snide things against such priests, I can only pray that I learn better in another life. But today a man like me has little voice; his bad remarks, his rudeness toward others, matter little (except before God), because there is no one to hear. Everyone listens to the men of outrage and alarm. Few pay much attention to the millions of Catholics all over the world who are not unlike my own parishioners—or to priests like me, who are so quickly dismissed as out-of-date.

"I may sound as if I am asking for pity or attention— or both! At my age, though, a man loses a bit of the vanity we are all heir to. It is dangerous, I know, for one like me to make such a judgment, but I will take the risk. I am simply asking that 'the people' be heard— a cry worthy of a reformer, even an agitator! I do not mean that we limit our vision to their vision. Those of us in a position to lead should try to lead; it is sad to see leaders justifying their own prejudices and inertia by pointing out the presence of both in 'the people.' But it is also sad to see leaders lose touch with their followers, or those supposed to be their followers. And some leaders are self-appointed, and speak for audiences or groups other than the ones they claim to be from, or working for.

"I have nothing more to say. I have been held back by the climate here—so cold in winter, so hot in summer —I occasionally say to myself in justification for my lethargy. At other times I feel that I have done my best. And then there are those moments when I have to confess to myself: I have been a coward, even as so many of my superiors in the Church have betrayed Christ. But I love being here, and have been privileged to earn a certain place here, a certain measure of affection and respect from people I have grown to care for and love, for all their failures and blindness. I am old, and I suppose it is the old Church I represent. I am Spanish, and so I have a streak of the mystical in me, and a streak of indifference—I should admit it—to all that is new and yeasty. I tend to fold my hands and say that this too will pass, and afterwards there will be the same problems: those with power and those with much less; those who live better than others; those who die young and the old, grouchy ones like myself who hold on to life longer than seems fair, considering all the children who are doomed by fate. So it was in Christ's time; and the Spanish Church has never been inclined to think it will be much different any time this side of Armageddon.

"But I am American, so if I am of the Spanish Church, I am also of the American Church: I may dislike a lot of changes I see these days (the television set my parishioners bought me!) but I am also glad that there is a lot of ferment in this country; and there are even times when I wish I could lose all this weight and shed my wrinkles and gain back the energy I had, in order to go picket somewhere! Maybe more important to gain back than the energy would be anger: good, clean anger at the rich and powerful, the self-contented and the hypocritical. Americans are always looking for solutions, answers; they are—we are—so restless, and so taken up with ourselves. It is a bad trait—the danger of pride; it is a good trait—the courage to change, the strength to oppose what is wicked but entrenched. Don't ask me to give percentages of how much bad, how much good. When one is old one tends to rest with the oars; when one is young, one has one's eye on new goals. Perhaps the Spanish Church is old, the American young. As for me, I am half and half. What I know without question is that I have given up searching for consistency. My mother influenced me a lot, but one thing she taught me I no longer believe:

consistency is *not* a virtue. Or, I should say this: it is not a virtue I will ever possess."

His eyes now look to his visitor, then through the window to some cattle moving down the road, followed by a young man on horseback. The cattle are wandering all over, and the man is trying to hold them together. Behind him are cars: one, two, three—a line of them. The man seems not to notice them, let alone show any signs of hurrying his herd. Finally, one driver loses his patience and honks his horn which gives the other drivers courage to do likewise. Now the man angrily stops his horse: he will leave the cattle to their own devices; he will stay there all day if necessary; he will make his point. The priest is amused. It is not the first time he has witnessed such a confrontation, nor is it likely to be the last. Yet, each time he wonders what to think. Who is in the right? The man on horse is stubborn, maybe a bit spiteful. Still, he was there first, and the cattle have to be moved to another pasture, and they, too, belong to the town. The drivers probably don't; they are coming through to look, enjoy, feel a tinge of awe or envy—but soon enough they will leave, glad to be on their way to some city, some other part of the country, where they can talk about "the beauty of New Mexico," but live their more urbane, sophisticated, progressive lives.

A shrug of the priest's shoulders, another sigh; the protagonists have moved up the road and out of sight. He must prepare for tomorrow. He has confessions to hear. He has homes to visit. He is heavy and gets short of breath, but he is a walker: the families within two or so miles are reached on foot. As for the rest, he asks for help from young people who have cars. He enjoys driving with them; they are so full of joy and enthusiasm: the noise of the motor, the speed, the quick stop that defies the worst expectations of older

103

people. Sometimes he wishes he had learned to drive. Sometimes he has pictured himself at the wheel, going along at a fast rate, waving at his many friends. Younger priests do so many things he has not done, and it is good they do them, he knows. Nevertheless, when he comes back from a drive he is not only refreshed but pleased to take a walk, or simply sit and doze, or read— or else do something else: "Occasionally I sneak into the church, when I know no one is there. I sit at the very back; and to be honest, my mind doesn't do much. I'm not praying. I'm not thinking very hard. I just say a word or two to our Savior: 'It is up to You to make sense of all this; all we can do is try to be as upright as possible until we are summoned—and told how well we have done, or how badly.' Then I am ready to go outside and pick up again: the next obligation."